MY
INDIAN
BUCKET LIST
COOKBOOK

TANDOORI CHICKEN
(PAGE 103)

MY INDIAN BUCKET LIST COOKBOOK

60 Bold, Authentic Dishes
Everyone Needs to Try

NEHA MATHUR
creator of
Whisk Affair

PAGE STREET
PUBLISHING CO.

First published in 2022 by
Page Street Publishing Co.
27 Congress Street, Suite 105
Salem, MA 01970
www.pagestreetpublishing.com

Distributed by Macmillan, sales in Canada by The Canadian Manda Group.

25 24 23 22 21   1 2 3 4 5

ISBN-13: 978-1-64567-482-5
ISBN-10: 1-64567-482-7

Library of Congress Control Number: 2021937031

Cover and book design by Kylie Alexander for Page Street Publishing Co.
Photography by Neha Mathur

Printed and bound in United States

TO MY FAMILY

POTATO PEA SAMOSA
(PAGE 104)

CONTENTS

FOREWORD

There is nothing you can't achieve if you put your mind to it, and if working toward it brings you joy then the journey is super sweet. That, in a nutshell, is Neha's approach. She is a very inspiring and passionate personality, and her ambitious work compiling Indian food for the world to cook is commendable.

Cooking Indian food at home can be really daunting to many; I understand that. But with this book, Neha has put together a treasure of recipes that anyone can cook. Her book is a collection of classic finger-licking Indian food that you can cook at home, anywhere in the world. I wish her the best and definitely recommend readers to take a bite out of her recipes soon.

Chef Kunal Kapur

INTRODUCTION

Thanks for picking up this book and showing interest in Indian cuisine. If you are from India, I'm sure you have a natural taste for Indian food, and if you are trying Indian recipes for the first time, you are going to fall in love with cooking them. Throughout my professional life, I've come across people from various nationalities; many of them have now become good friends. When I look back, I can see that we have connected on common areas of interest, including food. I'm surprised at how many of them loved Indian cuisine. Some of them have even thanked me for introducing them to Indian cooking for the first time.

Rasoi in India means "kitchen" and through this book, I want to bring my rasoi closer to you. Here, you will find recipes that can be prepared easily in your kitchen using basic equipment. My selection of recipes for this bucket list was to give you local must-have flavors from different regions of India; cooking these recipes will quickly immerse you in a broad range of Indian cuisine, introducing foods and spices that will give you a newfound love for Indian dishes, perhaps even those with which you consider yourself familiar. Every recipe offers a burst of flavors that will check all the boxes on your bucket list of Indian dishes.

While I love to cook now, you would be surprised to know that I never cooked as a kid; in fact, I didn't cook until I got married. I started from the very basics. I still remember starting with a simple rice recipe, something that my mom dictated to me over a phone call. I wrote down the proportion of rice and water in a diary—I used it many times over.

This diary continued to be my cooking bible as I jotted down many more recipes from my family and friends. I also remember buying several Indian magazines that always had a few printed recipes. I used to tear out the relevant recipe pages and got them bound together in book shops so I could refer to them whenever I made them.

What I learned in my early years of cooking was that in every recipe it is essential to maintain the correct proportions. I've continued with this mantra of writing down recipes once they turn out well and reuse them many times over. All these tried and tested recipes also helped me launch my blog, Whisk Affair, in 2012 and share them with my readers so everyone can get the best taste. My blog has since grown to 1,000+ recipes from India and across the globe.

My goal with this book is for people to experience Indian cuisine with ease. I've picked recipes you must try and those that can be made with little effort in a home kitchen. Each of the recipes in this book has been personally tested for the proportions of the ingredients and cooking instructions, so rest assured that it will turn out well. Each mouthwatering image that you see in this book is how the recipe turned out, and I personally shot all of them. If you love Indian cuisine, this is the book for you.

You can write to me, ask me questions, send me pictures of your dishes and tell me stories of how your friends and family loved the dishes at neha@whiskaffair.com. Let's get started and get cooking!

Neha

ALOO PANEER KOFTA (PAGE 36)

MY FAVORITE VEGETARIAN CURRIES

I still remember my childhood when I used to accompany my dad to the local *mandis*. In India, mandis are large groups of stalls selling vegetables ranging from the regular staples of onions, potatoes and tomatoes to green and seasonal vegetables at a reasonable price. This was a weekly routine for most of us growing up in India, and I've continued this tradition to this day.

Did you know India has a large number of vegetarians? The recent count suggests that it is more than in the rest of the world put together. No wonder a large variety of vegetarian dishes are made in India. You will also find many vegetarian restaurants in India as well as many vegetarian Indian restaurants around the world. These dishes can be super comforting, like 10-Minute Rasedar Aloo (potato curry; page 22) or Dal Fry (page 35), or you could indulge and make something rich and creamy like India's Most Favorite Paneer Makhani (page 14), Dhaba-Style Dal Makhani (page 18) or Navratan Korma (page 31). I've also experimented over time with mixing many vegetables with legumes, including lentils, chickpeas and so on. The likes of chickpeas cooked with spinach (Chana Saag [page 25]) bring them together in an interesting way.

When you are trying out Indian cuisine, you must try these vegetarian main course recipes. Make Kadhi Pakora (page 29) for a relaxing meal or Handi Paneer (page 26) and Shahi Mix Vegetables (page 39) for a party; this selection will surely make you fall in love with Indian cuisine.

INDIA'S MOST FAVORITE PANEER MAKHANI

SERVES 4

A delectable and luscious curry is something I always look for whenever I host a dinner for my near and dear ones. If we talk about rich vegetarian curries, this recipe is definitely a keeper–pieces of *paneer* dunked in a smooth and rich tomato cashew curry. I feel this curry has a royal touch to it, making it perfect to prepare for festive meals. If you have tried this curry in your favorite North Indian restaurant and are craving the same, then this recipe will surely excite you. One bite of naan with this oh-so-delicious paneer makhani and this will be your new favorite recipe.

In a nonstick 9-inch (23-cm) skillet, heat 1 tablespoon (14 g) of the butter and the oil over medium heat. Once the butter is melted, add the cloves and black and green cardamom pods, and sauté for 3 to 4 seconds, or until their flavor has seeped into the oil and butter. Add the red onion and sauté for 3 to 4 minutes, or until it is translucent. Add the tomato, ginger, garlic and green chile and sauté, stirring a few times, for 2 minutes. Add the cashews and cook for another 2 minutes.

Remove the pan from the heat and let the mixture cool completely. Once cooled, transfer it to a blender. Add ¼ cup (60 ml) of water and blend to a smooth masala paste.

Melt the remaining 3 tablespoons (42 g) of butter in the same nonstick pan over medium heat. Add the masala paste along with the coriander, turmeric, Kashmiri red chile powder, tomato paste, ketchup and salt to taste. Add ½ cup (120 ml) of water and mix everything well. Cook until the oil starts to separate on the sides of the pan, 8 to 10 minutes. You can cover the pan while cooking if the mixture is spattering too much.

Finally, add the paneer cubes, garam masala, cream, Cheddar cheese, honey and kasuri methi, and mix to coat the paneer with the masala in the pan. Cook the curry for another 2 minutes. Add more water if you want to thin out the curry. Garnish with swirls of cream and serve hot with Chile Cheese Naan.

NOTES

Kashmiri red chile powder gives an appetizing red color to the recipe and is mild in taste.

Kasuri methi is dried fenugreek; it adds a strong aroma and taste to Indian curries. You can buy them both from an Indian store or online on Amazon.

4 tbsp (½ stick, 56 g) unsalted butter, divided

1 tbsp (15 ml) vegetable oil

3 whole cloves

1 black cardamom pod

2 green cardamom pods

1 cup (160 g) chopped red onion

1 cup (180 g) chopped tomato

1 tsp chopped fresh ginger

2 tsp (7 g) chopped garlic

2 tsp (4 g) chopped green chile pepper

20 unsalted cashews

2 tsp (4 g) ground coriander

½ tsp ground turmeric

2 tsp (4 g) Kashmiri red chile powder (see Notes)

2 tbsp (32 g) tomato paste

3 tbsp (40 g) ketchup

Salt

1 lb (454 g) paneer, cut into 1" (2.5-cm) cubes

½ tsp garam masala spice blend

¼ cup (60 ml) heavy cream, plus more for garnish

¼ cup (30 g) shredded Cheddar cheese

1 tsp honey

2 tbsp (4 g) kasuri methi (see Notes)

1 recipe Chile Cheese Naan (page 87), for serving

PINDI CHANA (THE QUINTESSENTIAL PUNJABI CHICKPEA CURRY)

SERVES 4

Have you ever cooked a scrumptious chickpea curry at home? I am sure you must have, but have you ever tried this Punjabi *pindi chana*, which comes straight from the city of Rawalpindi, situated in the erstwhile Punjab province? Yes, pindi chana gets its name from this city and is also known as *pindi chole*. Well, if you have never had this spicy and tangy curry, then you are missing something super delicious. Its tempting flavor from freshly roasted masala and the dark brown color that comes from the black tea bag make pindi chana so tasty that you will wipe your dinner plate clean.

In a mortar and pestle, coarsely crush the cloves, black and green cardamom pods and cinnamon stick. In a heavy-bottomed 9-inch (23-cm) skillet with a tight-fitting lid (you will need it later), heat the oil over high heat until hot, add the crushed spices and fry them for 2 to 3 seconds. They will release all their aromas and flavors into the oil and make the curry very delicious. Add the onion, lower the heat to medium and cook, stirring occasionally, until the onion turns golden brown, 8 to 10 minutes. If the onion is getting dry as it cooks, add a few splashes of water to prevent it from sticking to the pan and burning.

Once the onion turns a light golden color, add the ginger-garlic paste and cook for 2 minutes. Add the tomato and cook for another minute. Add the chole masala, coriander, Kashmiri red chile powder, turmeric, cumin and mango powder, and fry until the oil starts to separate from the sides of the pan, 4 to 5 minutes.

Now, add the chickpeas along with their liquid, salt to taste and 2 cups (480 ml) of water. Mix everything well. Add the black tea bag, cover the pan, lower the heat to medium-low and cook for 10 to 12 minutes. Open the lid, and using tongs, remove the tea bag from the curry. Mash the chickpeas lightly, using the back of a ladle. This extra step of mashing chickpeas will make sure the curry is super creamy. Finally, add the kasuri methi and mix well. Serve hot with poori.

NOTE

Dried mango powder is made from green mangoes and is also known as amchur powder. It should be available in an Indian store or online.

4 whole cloves

1 black cardamom pod

2 green cardamom pods

1 (1" [2.5-cm]) piece cinnamon stick

¼ cup (60 ml) vegetable oil

1 cup (160 g) grated red onion

2 tsp (5 g) ginger-garlic paste

1 cup (180 g) grated tomato

2 tbsp (6 g) chole masala spice blend

1 tsp ground coriander powder

1 tsp Kashmiri red chile powder

½ tsp ground turmeric

1 tsp ground cumin

1 tsp dried mango powder (see Note)

1 (15-oz [425-g]) can chickpeas, undrained

Salt

1 black tea bag

1 tbsp (2 g) kasuri methi

Poori, for serving

DHABA-STYLE DAL MAKHANI

SERVES 4

The creamy texture, richness and beautiful aroma that lingers around the entire house when you cook this dish is definitely something to look forward to. A delicious combination of *urad dal* (black lentils), *chana dal* (Bengal gram) and *rajma* (red kidney beans), this lentil curry never fails to impress. Considered one of the most popular North Indian dals, it can be found in every possible restaurant. But I feel that homemade dal makhani is just out of this world and can surpass any restaurant's version. At home, you can always adjust the ingredients according to your taste and make it the way you like it. Do not compromise on the ghee, butter and cream, because these are the ingredients that make this dal *makhani*, which means "extra buttery and creamy." Due to its rich ingredients and royal taste, it is perfect to serve for your festive or special meals.

½ cup (96 g) dried black lentils

1 tbsp (10 g) Bengal gram

¼ cup (44 g) red kidney beans

1 to 1½ tsp (6 to 9 g) salt

¼ cup (56 g) ghee or clarified butter, divided

2 tsp (4 g) ginger-garlic paste

1 tsp Kashmiri red chile powder

½ tsp cumin seeds

1 cup (160 g) grated onion

1 tsp grated fresh ginger

¼ cup (70 g) tomato paste

1 tsp garam masala spice blend

2 tbsp (30 g) unsalted butter

¼ cup (60 ml) heavy cream, plus more for garnish

1 tbsp (2 g) kasuri methi

1 recipe Lachha Paratha (page 89), for serving

In a medium-sized bowl, combine the black lentils, Bengal gram and red kidney beans and rinse them well. Drain, then soak the mixture in 4 cups (960 ml) of fresh water for 8 to 10 hours at room temperature. Once soaked, drain the water and transfer the dal mixture to a 3-quart (3-L) stovetop pressure cooker along with the salt, 2 tablespoons (28 g) of the ghee, the ginger-garlic paste and the Kashmiri red chile powder. Add 5 cups (1.2 L) of fresh water to the cooker and close the lid. Pressure cook the dal over high heat until the first whistle sounds, then lower the heat to low and cook for 18 to 20 minutes.

Remove the pressure cooker from the heat and let the pressure release naturally. Once the pressure is released, open the lid of the cooker and mash the dal very well with the back of a ladle. The dal should become creamy at this stage with a few small pieces of lentils intact. If the dal is not getting creamy, you will have to pressure cook it for a little more time.

To temper the dal, in a large skillet, heat the remaining 2 tablespoons (28 g) of ghee over medium-high heat. Once the ghee is hot, add the cumin seeds and let them crackle for a few seconds. Lower the heat to medium, add the onion and cook until it turns slightly brown, 6 to 8 minutes. Add the ginger and tomato paste and cook, stirring regularly, for another 2 minutes.

Add the cooked dal to the pan along with the garam masala, butter, cream and kasuri methi, and mix everything well. Lower the heat to low and cook the dal, stirring and mashing it with the back of a ladle, for 10 to 12 minutes. Garnish with swirls of cream and serve with Lachha Paratha.

NOTE

To cook the dal in an Instant Pot®, combine the ingredients for pressure cooking in an Instant Pot, reducing the water measurement to 3 cups (720 ml). Pressure cook for 30 minutes at high pressure, followed by natural pressure release.

BHINDI FRY (OKRA FRY)

A quick and flavorful stir-fry is all you need for a healthy meal on a weekday. Don't you agree? A good Indian stir-fry, a bowl of *raita* and hot *roti*—I think this is a perfectly healthy and comforting meal for your workday. A lot of stir-fries are prepared in my kitchen on an everyday basis, but this *bhindi* fry is an all-time favorite. Okra is fried with a few common Indian spices to prepare this recipe. In fact, it's so easy to make that even a first-timer can make it perfectly. This recipe takes less than 30 minutes to cook.

10 oz (283 g) okra
¼ cup (60 ml) vegetable oil
2 dried red chiles
1 cup (160 g) sliced red onion
Salt
1 tsp ground coriander
1 tsp Kashmiri red chile powder
½ tsp ground turmeric
1 tsp dried mango powder
Poori or paratha, for serving

Wash the okra well with water and wipe each of them, using a paper towel. It's best to wash the okra one day before making the curry, to get rid of all the moisture. If the okra is moist while cooking, it will become slimy. Once dry, chop off and discard ½ inch (1.2 cm) from the top and bottom tips. Chop the remaining okra into ¼-inch (6-mm) rounds.

In a medium-sized, heavy-bottomed skillet with a tight-fitting lid (you will need it later), heat the oil over medium-high heat. Once the oil is hot, lower the heat to medium. Break the dried red chiles in half and add them to the hot oil. You can discard the seeds of the dried chiles before adding them to the oil if you want to keep the curry mild. Fry the chiles for 20 seconds. Add the red onion, increase the heat to medium-high and fry, stirring, until it turns golden brown, 8 to 10 minutes.

Once the onion is nicely browned, add the okra, salt to taste, coriander, Kashmiri red chile powder and turmeric, and mix everything well. Cover the pan and lower the heat to low. Cook, stirring occasionally, until the okra is softened, 10 to 15 minutes. Once the okra is softened and cooked well, add the dried mango powder and mix well. Serve hot with poori or paratha.

10-MINUTE RASEDAR ALOO

SERVES 4

What is your treasured weekend meal? Well, everyone at my home likes to enjoy a delicious bowl of *rasedar aloo* with some hot puffed poori and *boondi raita* on their plate. The mere glimpse of this rasedar aloo brings a subtle smile on their lazy weekend faces. Therefore, Sunday lunches are all about *aloo puri*, the most extraordinary Indian combination ever: soft, boiled potatoes dunked in a thin tomato-based curry flavored with some everyday spices. You will know the real joy of eating it when you take that first bite. Rasedar aloo is very common in Indian households, and let me tell you that every home has its own way of making it, too. But after trying several different recipes, I am hooked on this one. This recipe is super easy, quick and loaded with flavor. So, next time your family demands a plate of goodness, you know where to find it.

In a blender, combine the tomato, ginger and green chile and blend to a smooth puree. In a medium-sized skillet, heat the oil over medium heat. Once the oil is hot, add the asafetida and cumin seeds and let them crackle for a few seconds, stirring constantly. Add the tomato mixture and cook, stirring constantly, for 2 minutes over medium heat.

Now, add the coriander seeds, fennel, turmeric, Kashmiri red chile powder and garam masala, and cook, stirring frequently, until the oil separates from the sides of the pan, 2 to 3 minutes. Using your fingers, crush the boiled potatoes into small pieces and add them to the pan. Add 2 cups (480 ml) of hot water, the dried mango powder and salt to taste, and cook for 3 to 4 minutes, or until the curry comes to a boil.

The consistency of the curry should be watery. If you would like to thin the curry further, add some more water and cook for another minute. Garnish with fresh cilantro and serve hot with poori.

1 cup (180 g) chopped ripe tomato

1 (1" [2.5-cm]) piece fresh ginger, chopped

2 tsp (4 g) chopped green chile

3 tbsp (45 ml) vegetable oil

½ tsp asafetida

1 tsp cumin seeds

2 tsp (4 g) coarsely crushed coriander seeds

1 tsp ground fennel

½ tsp ground turmeric

2 tsp (4 g) Kashmiri red chile powder

½ tsp garam masala spice blend

1 lb (454 g) potatoes, boiled and peeled

1 tsp dried mango powder

Salt

2 tbsp (4 g) chopped fresh cilantro, for garnish

Poori, for serving

CHANA SAAG

Saag is a gluten-free winter favorite that is prepared in Punjabi homes. It could be made with different leaves; however, spinach is the most prominent one. To give it a different flavor, I often add chickpeas. This *chana saag*—chickpeas cooked in spinach leaf curry—is a delicious way to include protein and iron in your everyday meals at the same time. Soft, boiled chickpeas added to a creamy and thick curry made with pureed spinach cooked with spicy tomato and onion masala, this chana saag is a must-try Indian curry.

¼ tsp baking soda

7 oz (198 g) spinach

2 green chiles

¼ cup (60 ml) vegetable oil

1 tsp cumin seeds

2 dried red chiles

1 cup (160 g) finely chopped onion

6 cloves garlic, crushed

1 cup (180 g) finely chopped tomato

2 tsp (4 g) ground coriander

½ tsp garam masala spice blend

1 (15-oz [425-g]) can chickpeas, undrained

Salt

2 tsp (10 ml) fresh lime juice

2 tbsp (30 ml) heavy cream, plus more for garnish

Naan or paratha, for serving

In a large pot, heat 6 cups (1.4 L) of water over high heat. Once the water comes to a boil, add the baking soda and spinach and cook for 2 minutes. After 2 minutes, drain the water and run the spinach under cold water immediately. This step is called blanching; it cooks the spinach and retains its beautiful green color and nutrients. Baking soda is added to the water to retain the color even more. Transfer the drained spinach to a blender along with the green chiles and blend to a smooth paste. Set this paste aside.

To make the curry, in a medium-sized skillet, heat the oil over medium-high heat. Once the oil is hot, add the cumin seeds and dried red chiles and let them crackle for a few seconds. Add the onion and garlic and fry until the onion turns translucent, 5 to 6 minutes. Add the tomato and cook, stirring regularly, for 3 to 4 minutes. I like my saag chunky and so I do not blend it, but if you like smooth saag, you can blend the mixture at this stage, using an immersion blender, for a creamier curry.

Now, add the coriander and garam masala to the pan and fry for another minute. Add the spinach paste that you made earlier, increase the heat to high and sauté for a minute. Add the chickpeas along with their liquid, salt to taste and ½ cup (120 ml) of water and bring the curry to a boil. Turn off the heat, add the lime juice and cream and mix well. Garnish the chana saag with swirls of cream and serve hot with naan or paratha.

HANDI PANEER

Handi paneer is a delicious and creamy paneer curry that is cooked in a *handi*, a type of clay pot that has a shallow depth and a wide bottom. If you do not have this kind of pot, you can make it in a wok, *kadai* or heavy-bottomed skillet. This paneer curry gets its creamy texture from cashews, which are mixed in the spicy tomato and onion masala. Overall, this rich handi paneer is a must-try for anyone who loves Indian cuisine!

Make the masala paste: In a small food processor, combine all the masala paste ingredients with ¼ cup (60 ml) of water. Process to a smooth paste.

Make the curry: In a handi or medium-sized, heavy-bottomed skillet, heat the oil over medium-high heat. Once the oil is hot, add the bay leaves, peppercorns, cloves, cinnamon stick and green cardamom pod, and fry them for a few seconds to release all their flavor into the oil. Add the onion and fry, stirring regularly, until the onion is dark brown, 10 to 12 minutes; take care to not let the onion burn. Once the onion is well browned, add the Kashmiri red chile powder and turmeric and fry for just 2 to 3 seconds. Do not overcook; otherwise, the spices will burn. Add the masala paste that you made earlier and cook, stirring, for 4 to 5 minutes, or until the oil starts to separate from the sides of the pan.

Now, add the paneer cubes, salt to taste, kasuri methi and cilantro and mix everything well. Add ½ cup (120 ml) of warm water and cook for another minute. Serve with Lachha Paratha.

MASALA PASTE

2 dried red chiles

1 tbsp (5 g) coriander seeds

1 tsp cumin seeds

1 tsp fennel seeds

10 cashews

½ cup (90 g) chopped tomato

1 tsp chopped fresh ginger

2 cloves garlic, peeled

CURRY

¼ cup (60 ml) vegetable oil

2 bay leaves

4 black peppercorns

2 whole cloves

1 (1" [2.5-cm]) piece cinnamon stick

1 green cardamom pod

1 cup (160 g) chopped onion

2 tsp (4 g) Kashmiri red chile powder

½ tsp ground turmeric

10 oz (283 g) paneer, cut into cubes

Salt

1 tbsp (2 g) kasuri methi

2 tbsp (4 g) chopped fresh cilantro

1 recipe Lachha Paratha (page 89), for serving

KADHI PAKORA (MY TREAT FROM CHILDHOOD)

SERVES 4

Kadhi pakora served with *chawal* (rice) is one of the most quintessential North Indian combos ever! While growing up, this was a treat we used to look forward to. You can serve it any day of the week. Many times, my mom still brings me a bowl full of kadhi pakora when she comes over for a meal.

It is easy to spot this combo being served in many *dhabas* (roadside eateries) and fine restaurants. Sour yogurt and chickpea flour are combined together to make this delectable kadhi cooked with curry leaves, mustard seeds, fenugreek seeds and other flavorings. If you haven't enjoyed a bowl of warm and comforting kadhi pakora yet, it's high time you tried this recipe.

Make the kadhi: In a medium-sized bowl, whisk the yogurt, using a wire whisk, until smooth and creamy. Add the chickpea flour and whisk well to make a smooth, lump-free paste. Add 3 cups (720 ml) of water and mix well until combined, then set aside. In a medium-sized skillet, heat the oil over medium-high heat. Once the oil is hot, add the fenugreek seeds, mustard seeds, cumin seeds, curry leaves and asafetida to the pan and let them crackle, stirring, for 2 to 3 seconds. Then, add the chickpea flour mixture that you made earlier and mix well. Add the turmeric, Kashmiri red chile powder and salt to taste, and bring the mixture to a boil. Once the mixture comes to a boil, lower the heat to low and cook the kadhi for 20 minutes, or until it thickens. Add the lime juice and stir well.

Make the pakora: In a small bowl, stir together the chickpea flour, salt and baking powder. Add 2 tablespoons (30 ml) of water, 1 tablespoon (15 ml) at a time, and mix to make a thick batter. Pour enough oil into a shallow skillet to fill the pan by 1 inch (2.5 cm) and heat over medium-high heat. Once the oil is hot, lower the heat to low. Drop the batter, 1 teaspoon at a time, into the oil, spacing the pakora 1 inch (2.5 cm) apart. The pakora will puff up slightly above the oil. After 3 to 4 minutes of frying, flip the pakora onto the other side, using a slotted spoon, and fry for another 3 to 4 minutes, or until they turn slightly brown on all sides. Using the slotted spoon, remove the pakora from the hot oil and then add them to the hot kadhi.

(continued)

KADHI

½ cup (120 g) plain yogurt
½ cup (70 g) chickpea flour
2 tbsp (30 ml) vegetable oil
½ tsp fenugreek seeds
1 tsp mustard seeds
1 tsp cumin seeds
10 curry leaves
¼ tsp asafetida
½ tsp ground turmeric
1 tsp Kashmiri red chile powder
Salt
1 tsp fresh lime juice

PAKORA

½ cup (70 g) chickpea flour
¼ tsp salt
⅛ tsp baking powder
Oil, for frying

Once the kadhi and pakora are ready, give the kadhi a tempering: In a small skillet, heat the ghee over medium-high heat. Once the ghee is hot, add the broken dried red chiles and fry for 2 seconds. Remove the pan from the heat and add the Kashmiri red chile powder. Immediately pour the tempering over the kadhi. Be quick after adding the Kashmiri red chile powder to the hot oil; otherwise, it may burn. Serve with the pakora.

NOTE

You can add thinly sliced onion, chopped spinach and so on to the pakora batter before frying to get a different flavor.

FOR TEMPERING

2 tbsp (30 g) ghee

3 dried red chiles, broken into 2 pieces

½ tsp Kashmiri red chile powder

NAVRATAN KORMA

Navratan korma, the name of this royal dish, is significant enough for you to understand what it really stands for! Here, *nav* means "nine" and *ratan* means "jewels," which means this Indian dish is prepared with nine jewels (ingredients, which can be a combination of fruits, vegetables and nuts), cooked in a super rich and creamy base prepared with cashews and poppy seeds, and finished with heavy cream. Some people even add almonds and melon seeds to boost the richness of the curry. Since navratan korma is a combination of fruits, nuts and cream, it is on a sweeter side and not at all spicy. The nine main ingredients used in the following recipe are potato, carrot, cauliflower, green beans, green peas, paneer, fox nuts, red apple and pomegranate seeds. So, if you are someone who prefers sweet curries, this one is definitely for you. It is said that navratan korma was named after the nine courtiers in King Akbar's court, with the nine royal ingredients representing the courtiers. Interesting, isn't it? Well, for now, enjoy this sweet Indian curry.

Make the paste: In a small bowl, soak the almonds, cashews, poppy seeds and melon seeds in ½ cup (120 ml) of room-temperature water for 15 minutes. Transfer the soaked nuts along with the water to a blender and blend to a smooth paste. Set the paste aside.

Blanch the vegetables: In a large pot, heat 6 cups (1.4 L) of water over high heat. Once the water comes to a boil, add the sugar to it. Sugar helps keep the color of the veggies vibrant. Add the potato, carrot, cauliflower, green beans and green peas, and cook them for 30 seconds. Then, drain the water and transfer the vegetables to a bowl filled with ice-cold water. Let the vegetables sit in the cold water for 2 to 3 minutes, then drain and set aside. This process cooks the veggies and retains their nutrients and color.

Make the curry: In a medium-sized skillet, heat the ghee and oil over medium-high heat. Once they are hot, add the paneer cubes and fry them, turning the cubes to cook evenly, until they are browned on all sides, 3 to 4 minutes. Once browned, remove the paneer pieces, using a ladle, and place in a separate bowl filled with water. This will ensure the paneer is soft and tender and not chewy.

Add the fox nuts to the same pan and fry, stirring, until they are crisp, 2 to 3 minutes, then remove them with a ladle and transfer to a plate.

Next, add the green cardamom pods, cloves, cinnamon stick and bay leaves to the same pan and fry for a few seconds. Add the onion and fry, stirring, until it turns slightly brown, 8 to 10 minutes. Then, add the ginger-garlic paste and green chile and fry for another 2 to 3 minutes. The raw smell of ginger-garlic paste should go away.

(continued)

PASTE

¼ cup (36 g) almonds

¼ cup (36 g) cashews

2 tbsp (18 g) poppy seeds

2 tbsp (16 g) melon seeds (see Note)

VEGETABLES

1 tsp sugar

½ cup (75 g) peeled and cubed potato

½ cup (64 g) peeled and cubed carrot

1 cup (100 g) cauliflower florets

½ cup (55 g) chopped green beans (1" [2.5-cm] pieces)

½ cup (67 g) green peas

CURRY

2 tbsp (30 g) ghee

2 tbsp (30 ml) vegetable oil

4 oz (113 g) paneer, cut into 1" (2.5-cm) cubes

1 cup (10 g) fox nuts (see Note)

2 green cardamom pods

2 whole cloves

1 (1" [2.5-cm]) piece cinnamon stick

2 bay leaves

1 cup (160 g) sliced onion

2 tsp (10 g) ginger-garlic paste

2 tsp (4 g) chopped green chile

Now, add the Kashmiri red chile powder and turmeric and fry for 2 to 3 seconds. In a small bowl, whisk the yogurt with the flour, then add the mixture to the pan. Adding the flour to the yogurt makes sure it doesn't curdle while cooking and also makes the curry creamier. Cook for another 2 minutes. Add the paste that you made earlier along with ½ cup (120 ml) of water and cook for another minute.

Add the blanched vegetables, fried paneer, fried fox nuts, cubed apple and pomegranate seeds to the pan. Add ½ cup (120 ml) of water, lower the heat to low and cook until the vegetables are just tender, 5 to 6 minutes. You don't want the vegetables to get mushy. Once the vegetables are just cooked, add the cream, saffron and its milk, cardamom, garam masala and sugar, and mix well. Remove the pan from the heat.

Once the curry is ready, give it a tempering (this process is optional, so you can choose to skip it). In a medium-sized pan, heat the ghee over medium-high heat. Once the ghee is hot, add the almonds, cashews, pistachios and walnut halves and fry, stirring constantly with a small spoon, until they turn brown, about a minute. Once the nuts are browned, add the raisins and melon seeds and fry for another few seconds. Add the chopped pineapple, mint leaves and ginger and fry for 20 seconds. Pour the tempering over the cooked curry. Serve the navratan korma with Chile Cheese Naan.

NOTE

Melon seeds and fox nuts (also known as popped lotus seeds) should be available in an Indian store near you or on Amazon. If you are unable to get them, then just skip adding them.

1 tsp Kashmiri red chile powder

½ tsp ground turmeric

½ cup (120 g) plain yogurt

1 tsp all-purpose flour

½ cup (80 g) peeled, seeded and cubed red apple

¼ cup (20 g) pomegranate seeds

¼ cup (60 ml) heavy cream

20 strands saffron, soaked in 1 tbsp (15 ml) milk

1 tsp ground cardamom

1 tsp garam masala spice blend

1 tsp sugar

FOR TEMPERING

1 tbsp (15 g) ghee

5 almonds

5 cashews

5 unsalted pistachios

5 walnut halves

10 raisins

1 tsp melon seeds (see Note)

¼ cup (50 g) peeled and cubed pineapple

10 fresh mint leaves

1 tsp julienned fresh ginger

1 recipe Chile Cheese Naan (page 87), for serving

DAL FRY

When it comes to Indian food, you can never have enough dal recipes. Dal, or lentils, being one of the staple foods in India, is prepared on an everyday basis for meals. There are a lot of variations you can make at home using different types of lentils. But some dal recipes are exceptional, and this dal fry is definitely one of them. Prepared using *toor dal* (pigeon peas), it is an extremely simple dal that gets its makeover with the *tadka* (tempering). The magical tadka of tomatoes, onion, ginger and garlic really brings out the delicious taste of this dal fry. I am sure you must have seen dal fry on the menu of almost all Indian restaurants. But why wait to go to a restaurant to enjoy your favorite dal, when you can make a better version at home. Right? So, follow this recipe, and you will have a beautifully flavored dal fry served right on your dining table.

1 cup (198 g) toor dal (pigeon peas)
½ tsp ground turmeric
1 to 1½ tsp (6 to 9 g) salt

FOR TEMPERING
2 tbsp (30 g) ghee
1 tbsp (15 ml) vegetable oil
1 tsp cumin seeds
¼ tsp asafetida
4 dried red chiles
2 tsp (6 g) chopped fresh ginger
2 tsp (7 g) chopped garlic
½ cup (80 g) chopped onion
2 tsp (5 g) chopped green chile
2 tsp (4 g) ground coriander
½ tsp ground turmeric
1 tsp Kashmiri red chile powder
½ cup (90 g) chopped tomato
2 tbsp (4 g) chopped fresh cilantro
1 tbsp (15 ml) fresh lime juice

Steamed rice, for serving

Wash the dal two times with water. Drain the water and place the dal in a pressure cooker along with 3½ cups (850 ml) of water, turmeric and salt. Close the lid of the cooker and pressure cook the dal over high heat until the first whistle sounds. Lower the heat to low and cook the dal for another 10 minutes. Remove the cooker from the heat and let the pressure release naturally. Once the pressure is released, open the lid of the cooker and whisk the dal well, using a wire whisk.

Make the tempering: In a medium-sized pan, heat the ghee and oil over medium-high heat. Once they are hot, add the cumin seeds and asafetida and fry for 3 to 4 seconds, or until they start to crackle. Add the dried red chiles, chopped ginger and garlic and fry for 2 minutes. Next, add the onion and green chile and fry for 4 to 5 minutes, or until the onion has browned. Then, add the coriander, turmeric and Kashmiri red chile powder and sauté for 3 to 4 seconds. Add the tomato and cilantro and cook for 4 to 5 minutes, or until the tomato is mushy. Now, add the cooked dal to the pan along with lime juice, and cook for 4 to 5 minutes. Serve hot with steamed rice.

NOTE

To make dal in an Instant Pot, combine the dal along with just 3 cups (720 ml) of water and the turmeric and salt in the Instant Pot, and cook on high pressure for 10 minutes followed by natural pressure release.

ALOO PANEER KOFTA

Kofta curry is one of the most popular Indian curries. Crispy on the outside and soft on the inside, aloo paneer koftas are dunked in a rich and creamy curry, which is definitely a treat for your taste buds. A variety of koftas can be dunked into the luscious creamy curry, but there is something about this recipe that is unbeatable. Potato and paneer, when combined, add a beautiful soft texture that no other ingredient can do. And when these koftas are added to the curry, it just elevates the overall taste of the dish.

Make the kofta: Grate the boiled potato, using the medium holes of a box grater, into a medium-sized bowl. Add the grated paneer, cornstarch, Kashmiri red chile powder, garam masala and salt to taste. Mix everything well to make a doughlike mixture. Make 1-inch (2.5-cm) balls from the dough. In a large pot, heat 4 cups (1 L) of oil over medium-high heat, for frying the kofta. Roll each of the kofta in the flour and place them in the hot oil. Reduce the heat to medium and fry the kofta, flipping them as they fry so they brown evenly, until browned from all sides, 6 to 8 minutes. Once browned, drain them on a plate lined with paper towels.

Make the curry: Heat a medium-size skillet over medium-high heat. Add 2 tablespoons (30 g) of the ghee to the pan. Once the ghee is hot, add the onion, ginger, garlic, green chiles and tomato to the pan. Increase the heat to high and sauté for 6 minutes. Add the cashews and fry for another 2 minutes. Then, remove the pan from the heat and let the mixture cool down to room temperature. Once the mixture has cooled completely, transfer it to a blender and blend to a smooth masala paste. Strain the masala paste through a fine-mesh sieve to get a silky, smooth curry. Discard the solids. Now, in the same pan, heat the remaining 2 tablespoons (30 g) of ghee over medium-high heat. Once the ghee is hot, add the Kashmiri red chile powder and turmeric and quickly sauté for 2 seconds, then immediately add the masala paste that you made earlier. Add ½ cup (120 ml) of water and salt to taste. Lower the heat to medium and cook the paste for about 10 minutes, or until the curry is slightly thickened. Finally, add the ketchup, cream and kasuri methi, and mix everything well. Cook for a minute.

To serve, put the kofta in a serving dish and pour the warm curry on top of the kofta. Garnish with swirls of cream (if using) and chopped cilantro, and serve immediately with Missi Roti.

NOTES

Test fry a kofta to check that they are not breaking in the oil. If they are, then add some more cornstarch to kofta mixture.

Pour the curry over the kofta only when you are ready to serve, for a fresh taste.

KOFTA

1 medium-sized (100 g) boiled potato

4 oz (113 g) paneer, grated

1 tbsp (8 g) cornstarch

¼ tsp Kashmiri red chile powder

¼ tsp garam masala spice blend

Salt

Oil, for frying

2 tbsp (16 g) all-purpose flour

CURRY

4 tbsp (60 g) ghee, divided

½ cup (80 g) sliced onion

2 tsp (4 g) chopped fresh ginger

2 tsp (7 g) chopped garlic

2 green chiles, slit in half

1 cup (180 g) chopped tomato

¼ cup (38 g) unsalted cashews

2 tsp (4 g) Kashmiri red chile powder

¼ tsp ground turmeric

Salt

2 tbsp (28 g) ketchup

¼ cup (60 ml) heavy cream

1 tbsp (2 g) kasuri methi

Heavy cream, for garnish (optional)

1 tsp fresh cilantro, for garnish

1 recipe Missi Roti (page 94), for serving

SHAHI MIX VEGETABLES

SERVES 6

Loaded with the goodness of vegetables, rich and creamy curry and out-of-this-world taste, this recipe is the answer to your dilemma of preparing something super delicious for your next Indian meal. *Shahi* means "royal," and *mix veg* is an Indian expression for "a combination of two or more vegetables," which means it is perfect for those memorable royal meals that are prepared to celebrate your special occasions. With this array of vegetables cooked in a delicious tomato, onion and cashew-based curry, the taste will linger on your tongue for long after you take a bite.

Fry the vegetables: In a medium-sized skillet, heat the oil over medium-high heat. Once the oil is hot, add the potatoes to the pan and fry them, stirring and turning them, until they are golden brown on all sides, 2 to 3 minutes. Once browned, transfer the potato cubes to a plate, using a ladle. Next, add the carrots, green beans and cauliflower florets to the same pan and fry them until they are browned and tender, 5 to 6 minutes. Transfer them to the same plate as the potatoes, using the ladle. Now, add the paneer cubes to the same oil and fry them until browned from all sides, 3 to 4 minutes. Once fried, transfer them to the plate of fried vegetables, using the ladle.

Make the curry: In a large skillet with a tight-fitting lid (you'll need it later), heat 1 tablespoon (16 g) of the butter and 1 tablespoon (15 ml) of the oil over medium-high heat. Once they are hot, add the onion, cashews, ginger, garlic, tomato and cubed potato to the pan. Lower the heat to medium and cook, stirring, for 5 to 6 minutes. Add 1 cup (240 ml) of water to the pan and cook, covered, for 10 minutes. Remove the pan from the heat, remove the lid and let the mixture cool down to room temperature. Transfer the cooled mixture to a food processor and process to make a smooth masala paste.

In a medium-sized skillet, heat 1 tablespoon (16 g) of the butter and the remaining tablespoon (15 ml) of oil over medium-high heat. Once they are hot, add the peas and bell pepper and cook them for a minute over high heat. Add the masala paste that you made earlier. Add the coriander, turmeric, Kashmiri red chile powder, salt to taste, garam masala, kasuri methi and cream to the pan. Mix everything well, lower the heat to medium and cook for 4 to 5 minutes. Finally add all the fried vegetables, ½ cup (120 ml) of water and the lime juice and mix everything well. Cook for another 3 to 4 minutes. Serve with naan or paratha.

VEGETABLES

1 cup (240 ml) oil, for frying

7 oz (198 g) potatoes, peeled and cubed

7 oz (198 g) carrots, peeled and cubed

4 oz (113 g) green beans, cut into 1" (2.5-cm) pieces

2 cups (200 g) cauliflower florets

4 oz (113 g) paneer, cut into 1" (2.5-cm) cubes

1 cup (145 g) green peas

4 oz (113 g) green bell pepper, cut into 1" (2.5-cm) pieces

CURRY

2 tbsp (¼ stick, 28 g) unsalted butter, divided

2 tbsp (30 ml) vegetable oil, divided

1 cup (160 g) chopped onion

¼ cup (36 g) cashews

2 tsp (4 g) chopped fresh ginger

2 tsp (7 g) chopped garlic

1 cup (180 g) chopped tomato

¼ cup (38 g) peeled and cubed potato

1 tsp ground coriander

½ tsp ground turmeric

2 tsp (4 g) Kashmiri red chile powder

Salt

½ tsp garam masala spice blend

1 tbsp (4 g) kasuri methi

2 tbsp (30 ml) heavy cream

1 tsp fresh lime juice

Naan or paratha, for serving

METHI FISH CURRY (PAGE 62)

MEAT- AND FISH-CENTRIC CURRIES

I cook a meat curry at home at least twice a week. Being from the northern part of India, for the longest time I've gorged on such delicacies as butter chicken and my dad's special kofta curry at home. We also enjoyed mutton, lamb, fish and egg curries made at home. However, once past my school days, I started to travel the length and breadth of India, where I found so many different varieties of these dishes from across various regions.

In this chapter, I've picked some of the most favorite Indian nonvegetarian curries. From Goan Lamb Vindaloo (page 44) to Keralan Coconut Milk Fish Curry (page 66), Mutton Sukka (page 47) from the Western Ghats to Anda Tawa Masala (page 65) from the north, and of course, one of the most widely ordered across the globe, Chicken Tikka Masala (page 43), you will have a good selection up your sleeve. Spices have played an important role in Indian cuisine. India is also one of the largest producers and consumers of spices. I'm sure with this book in your hand, you are wondering about how you can use spices in some of your curries. All of these recipes use spices in various combinations to bring out an authentic taste. Your proteins would never taste the same without these spices.

CHICKEN TIKKA MASALA

Chicken tikka masala is one of the most well-known Indian curries across the world. This is one of the first dishes that anyone new to Indian cuisine should try. A very mild chicken curry, it goes equally well with bread or rice. Marinated and grilled for incredible barbecue flavors, the chicken pieces just take the rich and creamy tomato-onion curry a notch level higher. This delicious chicken recipe is hard to ignore if you are looking to cook Indian cuisine. This specific recipe gives you authentic taste with juicy chicken tikka cubes, made in your home oven, which would easily rival those of your favorite Indian restaurant.

Pair it with naan or a bowl of Cumin Peas Pulao (page 71). Once you take a bite, the flavors will make you keep longing for more.

Make the chicken tikka: In a medium-sized bowl, combine all the chicken tikka ingredients and mix everything well to coat the chicken. Cover the bowl and refrigerate it for 10 to 12 hours. To cook, preheat the oven to 400°F (200°C). Transfer the marinated chicken pieces along with the marinade to a baking sheet and spread into a single layer. Bake for 20 to 22 minutes until the chicken is slightly charred on top. Remove the pan from the oven and set the tikka aside.

Make the curry: In a medium-sized skillet, heat the butter and oil over medium-high heat. Slightly crush the cardamom pods, cloves, cinnamon stick and peppercorns in a mortar and pestle, then add them to the pan. Let them crackle for 2 seconds. Lower the heat to medium, add the onion and fry until it turns translucent, 5 to 6 minutes. Add the ginger-garlic paste and fry for a minute. Next, add the chopped tomato and cook for 3 to 4 minutes, or until the tomato is mushy. Add the green chiles, tomato puree, Kashmiri red chile powder, turmeric, cumin, tikka masala spice and salt to taste, and cook for 3 to 4 minutes. Add the chicken that you baked earlier, along with ½ cup (120 ml) of water, and cook for 2 to 3 minutes. Now, add the cream, honey and kasuri methi to the pan and cook for another minute. Serve hot with Chile Cheese Naan or Cumin Peas Pulao.

NOTE

The tikka masala spice blend should be available in an Indian store near you or online on Amazon. If you can't find it, you can make your own blend by using the recipe on my blog.

CHICKEN TIKKA

1 lb (454 g) boneless chicken, cut into small cubes

¼ cup (62 g) Greek yogurt

2 tsp (6 g) ginger-garlic paste

1 tbsp (15 ml) fresh lime juice

2 tbsp (10 g) tikka masala spice blend (see Note)

2 tsp (11 g) salt

2 tbsp (30 ml) vegetable oil

CURRY

2 tbsp (30 g) unsalted butter

2 tbsp (30 ml) vegetable oil

2 green cardamom pods

4 whole cloves

1 (1" [2.5-cm]) piece cinnamon stick

4 black peppercorns

½ cup (60 g) finely chopped onion

1 tsp ginger-garlic paste

1 cup (180 g) finely chopped tomato

2 green chiles, slit in half

¼ cup (56 g) tomato puree

1 tsp Kashmiri red chile powder

½ tsp ground turmeric

½ tsp ground cumin

2 tbsp (10 g) tikka masala spice blend (see Note)

Salt

½ cup (120 ml) heavy cream

1 tbsp (15 ml) honey

2 tbsp (4 g) kasuri methi

1 recipe Chile Cheese Naan (page 87) or 1 recipe Cumin Peas Pulao (page 71), for serving

LAMB VINDALOO

My heart beams with joy whenever I visit Goa! You may be thinking, Why? Well, because what can be better than a Goan shack, fresh air, the sound of never-ending ocean waves and local vindaloo delicacy on your plate? Sounds perfect, doesn't it? Lamb vindaloo is a super spicy curry with a little tang, which is definitely a big hit among the locals as well as the tourists. Originally brought by the Goan Portuguese, vindaloo was traditionally prepared with pork. But when something tastes so delicious, you should try it with almost every substitute possible. And thus, vindaloo is now prepared with chicken, mutton, lamb, prawns and what-not. You name it and they will have it! But my favorite is lamb vindaloo. The juices from lamb go perfectly with the vindaloo curry. So, on the days when you crave a flavorful curry, this Goan lamb vindaloo is a perfect match. Want to make it even better? Serve it with steamed rice or naan and enjoy this scrumptious meal.

Make the vindaloo paste: Remove and discard the stalks from the dried chiles and soak them in the vinegar for 20 minutes. In a small skillet, combine the coriander seeds, cloves, cinnamon stick, green cardamom pods, peppercorns, cumin seeds and mustard seeds, and dry roast them over medium heat, stirring, until fragrant and slightly browned, 2 minutes. Remove from the heat. In a blender, combine the soaked chiles along with their vinegar, the roasted spices, plus the garlic, ginger, tamarind paste and ¼ cup (60 ml) of water and blend to a smooth paste. Set aside.

Make the curry: In a pressure cooker, heat the oil over medium-high heat. When the oil is hot, lower the heat to medium and add the red onion, stirring regularly, until golden brown, 10 to 12 minutes. Add the lamb pieces to the pressure cooker, increase the heat to high and fry, stirring occasionally, for 3 to 4 minutes, or until the lamb is lightly browned. Now, add the tomato puree, the vindaloo paste you made earlier, the turmeric, salt to taste and 1½ cups (360 ml) of water, and mix everything well.

(continued)

VINDALOO PASTE

10 dried Kashmiri red chiles (see Notes)

1 tbsp (15 ml) white vinegar

2 tbsp (10 g) coriander seeds

3 whole cloves

1 (1" [2.5-cm]) piece cinnamon stick

2 green cardamom pods

10 black peppercorns

1 tsp cumin seeds

1 tsp mustard seeds

5 cloves garlic, peeled

1 (1" [2.5-cm]) piece fresh ginger, peeled and chopped

1½ tbsp (50 g) tamarind paste

CURRY

6 tbsp (90 ml) vegetable oil

1½ cups (240 g) chopped red onion

1½ lb (680 g) lamb, with bones, cut into 1½" (4 cm) chunks

1 cup (225 g) tomato puree

1 tsp ground turmeric

Salt

½ tsp sugar

Steamed rice or naan, for serving

Close the lid of the pressure cooker and pressure cook over high heat until the first whistle sounds, then lower the heat to low. Cook for 12 to 15 minutes, then remove the pressure cooker from the heat. Let the pressure release naturally for about 10 minutes. Release any remaining pressure manually and open the lid of the pressure cooker.

Add the sugar and cook the curry, stirring, for another minute over low heat. Serve hot with steamed rice or naan.

NOTES

Reduce the number of chiles by half if you want the curry to be mild.

I used Kashmiri red chiles, which give this curry a fiery red color yet do not make it too spicy. You can use any chile that you are comfortable with.

Alternatively, you can cook the vindaloo in a regular pot instead of a pressure cooker. Add about 4 cups (950 ml) of water and cook the lamb mixture, covered, over low heat for at least 1½ hours, or until the meat becomes tender.

MUTTON SUKKA

This mutton *sukka* belongs to the Mangalore-Udupi area, along with the western India Konkan coast. This curry gets its deep red color from the dried red chiles grown in the region (Byadgi red chiles), which are known for their color and are not spicy. An ample amount of coconut and a few whole spices are used to give the dish a unique flavor. The aroma from the chiles, coconut and spices will fill your kitchen and make this dish even more appetizing. This sukka is a must-try dish from this region and goes perfectly with a flaky Lachha Paratha (page 89).

Dry roast the first group of ingredients: In a medium-sized skillet, combine the cumin seeds, coconut and garlic. Roast over medium heat, stirring constantly to prevent burning, until the coconut is slightly browned, 3 to 4 minutes. Once roasted, transfer the mixture to a plate and let cool completely. Once cooled, transfer the mixture to a small food processor or grinder and process to a smooth powder. Do not add water while processing. Transfer the dry-roasted masala powder to a bowl and set it aside.

Now, ghee-roast the next ingredients: In a medium-sized nonstick skillet, heat the ghee over medium-high heat. Once the ghee is hot, lower the heat to medium, add the coriander seeds, poppy seeds, fenugreek seeds, cinnamon stick, peppercorns, cloves and dried red chiles and roast, stirring constantly, until they are browned and fragrant, 3 to 4 minutes. Transfer the mixture to a plate and let cool completely. Once cooled, transfer the mixture to a blender. Add ½ cup (120 ml) of water and blend it into a smooth paste. Transfer the paste to a bowl and set it aside.

Make the curry: In a pressure cooker, heat the ghee over medium-high heat. Once the ghee is hot, add the onion and garlic and fry, stirring, until the onion turns translucent, 4 to 5 minutes. Add the goat mutton to the cooker, increase the heat to high and fry, stirring, for 3 to 4 minutes. Once the mutton is slightly browned, add the ghee-roasted masala paste that you made earlier. Add 1 cup (240 ml) of water and salt to taste, and close the lid of the cooker. Pressure cook over high heat until the first whistle sounds. Then, lower the heat to low and cook for 25 minutes, or until the mutton is tender. Remove the cooker from the heat and let the pressure release naturally. Once the pressure is released, open the lid of the cooker and check whether the mutton is tender. If not, pressure cook for another few minutes. Let the pressure release naturally and then open the cooker.

(continued)

FOR DRY ROASTING

1 tsp cumin seeds

1½ cups (110 g) grated fresh coconut

6 cloves garlic, peeled

FOR GHEE ROASTING

2 tbsp (30 g) ghee

3 tbsp (15 g) coriander seeds

1 tsp poppy seeds

¼ tsp fenugreek seeds

1 (1" [2.5-cm]) piece cinnamon stick

1 tsp black peppercorns

4 whole cloves

15 dried red chiles (see Notes)

CURRY

4 tbsp (60 g) ghee

1 cup (160 g) finely chopped onion

5 cloves garlic, crushed

2 lb (907 kg) goat mutton pieces, bone-in (see Notes)

Salt

1 tsp turmeric powder

2 tbsp (15 g) tamarind paste

Place the cooker over medium heat, add the dry-roasted masala powder that you made earlier and mix everything well. Cook the curry for another 10 to 12 minutes, or until the curry gets dry. Add the turmeric and tamarind paste, and cook for another 3 to 4 minutes.

Cook the tempering: In a medium-sized skillet, heat the ghee over medium-high heat. Add the onion and fry until browned, 3 to 4 minutes. Pour the tempering over the mutton. Serve hot with Lachha Paratha.

NOTES

Choose the dry red chiles that are mild with good color. You could reduce the amount to 5 if the chiles are not mild.

If goat mutton is not easily available to you, replace it with lamb.

Alternatively, to make this recipe in an Instant Pot, use the sauté setting to make the curry before closing the lid. Then, pressure cook on high pressure for 20 minutes, followed by natural pressure release.

FOR TEMPERING

2 tbsp (30 g) ghee

¼ cup (30 g) thinly sliced onion

1 recipe Lachha Paratha (page 89), for serving

FINGER-LICKING BUTTER CHICKEN

SERVES 4

Who doesn't love a delicious bowl filled with the ever-popular butter chicken, super creamy and rich with a slight tinge of sweetness? And when I say "rich," I mean it has an enormous amount of butter and fats, which makes it so irresistible. Due to its impeccable taste and perfect creamy texture, it has marked its place not only in India but all over the world. Preparing it and achieving the right taste and texture is an art that I'll show in very simple steps here. Roasted flavored chicken is added to a tomato and onion curry that gets its lusciousness from the use of cashews and fresh cream. At home, I love to serve it with naan or Cumin Peas Pulao (page 71).

Make the chicken: In a medium-sized bowl, mix all the chicken ingredients and let the chicken marinate for at least 2 to 3 hours in the refrigerator. It's best if you marinate it overnight.

Preheat the oven to 375°F (190°C). Arrange the chicken pieces in a single layer on a baking sheet lined with aluminum foil. Lining the pan with foil makes the cleanup easier. Roast the chicken for 25 minutes, or until nicely browned. Remove the pan from the oven and set it aside. Alternatively, you can grill the chicken in a grill pan or on a barbecue grill instead of in the oven.

Make the curry: In a pot, heat 4 cups (960 ml) of water to a boil. When it comes to a boil, add the cashews, tomato, onion, green and black cardamom pods, cinnamon stick, cloves and peppercorns, lower the heat to medium and cook for 10 minutes. Drain the water and transfer the boiled mixture to a blender. Add ¼ cup (60 ml) of water and blend to a smooth paste. Strain the paste through a fine-mesh strainer and set it aside.

In a medium-sized skillet, heat the butter over medium-high heat. When the butter is melted, add the Kashmiri red chile powder and fry for 1 to 2 seconds. Do not fry any longer; otherwise, the chile powder will burn. Add the cashew paste that you made earlier and stir well. Lower the heat to medium, add ½ cup (120 ml) of water to the pan and cook for 5 minutes, stirring regularly. Now, add salt to taste and the ketchup, khoya, Cheddar cheese, cream, kasuri methi, honey and lime juice, and cook for 2 minutes. Add the roasted chicken to the pan and adjust the consistency of the curry by adding more water, if needed. Cook for 2 minutes. Serve with Cumin Peas Pulao or naan.

NOTE

If you are not able to find khoya easily in a shop near you, use 2 tablespoons (15 g) of regular powdered milk mixed with 2 tablespoons (30 ml) of water.

CHICKEN

1½ lb (680 g) boneless chicken, cut into 1 inch (2.5 cm) pieces

2 tbsp (30 g) Greek yogurt

1 tsp ground coriander

2 tsp (4 g) Kashmiri red chile powder

2 tsp (6 g) ginger-garlic paste

1 tsp garam masala spice blend

1 tbsp (15 ml) fresh lime juice

1 tsp salt

CURRY

½ cup (75 g) cashews

1 cup (180 g) chopped tomato

½ cup (60 g) chopped onion

2 green cardamom pods

2 black cardamom pods

1 (1" [2.5-cm]) piece cinnamon stick

4 whole cloves

4 black peppercorns

3 tbsp (45 g) unsalted butter

2 tsp (4 g) Kashmiri red chile powder

Salt

2 tbsp (28 g) ketchup

2 oz (57 g) khoya, crumbled (see Note)

2 oz (57 g) Cheddar cheese, shredded

½ cup (120 ml) heavy cream

2 tbsp (4 g) kasuri methi

2 tbsp (40 g) honey

1 tbsp (15 ml) pure lime juice

1 recipe Cumin Peas Pulao (page 71) or naan, for serving

MUGHLAI EGG CURRY

SERVES 4

Mughlai cuisine comes from the kitchen of royal Mughals. Super aromatic, creamy and delectable, these recipes are known all over India for their incredible taste and flavor. It is said that Mughals used to love their curries. One such recipe is this legendary Mughlai egg curry made with boiled eggs. It will surely delight your taste buds for its richness and mild, aromatic flavors. Pair it with naan or Cumin Peas Pulao (page 71), for your extra-special meals.

Prepare the almonds and the eggs: Soak the almonds in ¼ cup (60 ml) of hot water for 15 minutes. Once soaked, remove and discard their skin and set the almonds aside. To prepare the eggs, peel the hard-boiled eggs and wipe them, using a paper towel. Make three or four slits in each egg, using a paring knife.

In a medium-sized skillet, heat the oil over medium-high heat. When the oil is hot, add the eggs to the pan, lower the heat to low and fry them, rotating them so that they brown evenly, until golden brown from all sides, 6 to 8 minutes. Once browned, transfer them to a plate and set them aside.

Add the ghee to the same pan and heat over medium-high heat. Once the ghee is hot, add the cloves, green cardamom pods and peppercorns, and fry for 4 to 5 seconds. Now, add the onion, ginger and garlic and fry, stirring regularly, until they turn golden brown, 10 to 12 minutes.

Once the onion mixture has browned, add the tomato and cook for another 3 to 4 minutes. Remove the pan from the heat and let the masala cool down for 15 minutes. Transfer the masala to a blender along with ¼ cup (60 ml) of water and the almonds and blend to a smooth paste. Transfer the paste to the same pan that was used to fry the masala. In a small bowl, whisk together the yogurt and flour. Adding a little flour to the yogurt will make sure it doesn't curdle while cooking. Add the yogurt mixture to the pan and cook for 30 seconds. Now, add the coriander, Kashmiri red chile powder, salt to taste, garam masala and 1 cup (240 ml) of water and mix everything well. Cook the curry for 5 to 6 minutes. Finally, add the saffron and its milk, kewra water and fried eggs to the curry, and bring to a boil. Add some more water if the curry looks very thick. Garnish with the cilantro and serve with naan or Cumin Peas Pulao.

NOTE

Kewra water is a fragrant Indian floral water that should be available in an Indian store near you or online on Amazon. It is also known as kewra essence.

10 almonds

6 hard-boiled large eggs

4 tbsp (60 ml) vegetable oil

3 tbsp (45 g) ghee

4 whole cloves

2 green cardamom pods

6 black peppercorns

1 cup (160 g) chopped onion

1 tsp chopped fresh ginger

2 tsp (7 g) chopped garlic

½ cup (180 g) chopped tomato

½ cup (120 g) plain yogurt

1 tsp all-purpose flour

1 tsp ground coriander

1 tsp Kashmiri red chile powder

Salt

½ tsp garam masala spice blend

10 to 12 strands saffron, soaked in 1 tbsp (15 ml) milk

3 to 4 drops kewra water (see Note)

1 tsp chopped fresh cilantro, for garnish

Naan or Cumin Peas Pulao (page 71), for serving

LAMB KORMA

A stew prepared with yogurt, aromatic whole spices and spice powders, this lamb dish offers authentic Indian flavors. It is a much milder curry as compared to others. *Korma* is a name that originated in the Mughal era; in local usage, it means "to combine everything together smoothly." Korma has been used in a number of both vegetarian and nonvegetarian recipes since then.

Lamb is generally cooked until tender and well done in Indian recipes; the softer it is, the more delicious it is in the curry. This popular dish from northern India has a simple method and delicious taste; you have to try this lamb korma recipe for your next meal.

Make the masala paste: In a medium-sized skillet, combine the cloves, cinnamon stick, peppercorns, green and black cardamom pods and cashews. Roast over medium heat, stirring constantly, until fragrant, 2 to 3 minutes.

Remove the pan from the heat and let the spices cool. Transfer the cooled spices to a blender along with the crispy fried onions. Add ¼ cup (60 ml) of water and blend to a smooth paste. Set the paste aside.

Make the curry: In a pressure cooker, heat the ghee and oil over high heat. Once they are hot, add the lamb pieces and fry, stirring frequently, for 5 to 6 minutes. Add the spice paste that you made earlier along with the ginger-garlic paste, lower the heat to medium and cook for 3 to 4 minutes. In a small bowl, whisk together the yogurt and flour. Adding a little flour to the yogurt will make sure it doesn't curdle while cooking. Now, add the yogurt mixture, coriander, Kashmiri red chile powder, turmeric, cumin and salt to taste, and fry for 3 to 4 minutes.

Add 2 cups (480 ml) of water, close the lid of the cooker, and pressure cook over high heat until the first whistle sounds. Lower the heat to low and cook for 20 to 25 minutes, or until the lamb is tender. Remove the cooker from the heat and let the pressure release naturally. Once the pressure is released, open the lid of the cooker and add the saffron and its water and the kewra water, and mix well. Add more water if you like the curry thinner and bring it to a boil. Serve with Lachha Paratha.

NOTE

Alternatively, to make this recipe in an Instant Pot, use the sauté setting to make the curry before closing the lid. Then, reducing the water measurement to 1½ cups (360 ml), pressure cook on high pressure for 20 minutes, followed by natural pressure release.

MASALA PASTE

6 whole cloves

1 (1" [2.5-cm]) piece cinnamon stick

6 black peppercorns

3 green cardamom pods

2 black cardamom pods

12 cashews

1 cup (180 g) crispy fried onions

CURRY

3 tbsp (45 g) ghee

3 tbsp (45 ml) vegetable oil

2 lb (907 g) lamb, bone-in

4 tsp (15 g) ginger-garlic paste

1 cup (245 g) plain yogurt

1 tbsp (8 g) all-purpose flour

2 tbsp (14 g) ground coriander

2 tsp (6 g) Kashmiri red chile powder

½ tsp ground turmeric

½ tsp ground cumin

Salt

12 strands saffron, soaked in 2 tbsp (30 ml) water

4 drops kewra water (see Note on page 53)

1 recipe Lachha Paratha (page 89), for serving

CHICKEN JALFREZI

If you're looking for slightly spicy chicken curry, then chicken *jalfrezi* is a perfect one to cook. Jalfrezi curries come from the state of West Bengal in India. Here, chicken is cooked in a rich, spicy onion and green bell pepper curry flavored with aromatic spices. A bowl of chicken jalfrezi on a bed of fragrant pulao and topped with some sliced onions is a perfectly satisfying meal that you can prepare for your dinner. It is easy, quick and delicious and is a great treat for your family.

In a medium-sized skillet, heat 2 tablespoons (30 ml) of the oil over medium-high heat. Once the oil is hot, add the sliced onion, bell pepper and garlic to the pan, increase the heat to high and stir-fry until the onion turns translucent, 2 to 3 minutes. Once the sliced onion is translucent, transfer it along with the bell pepper and garlic to a plate and set them aside. Heat the remaining 3 tablespoons (45 ml) of oil in the same pan over medium-high heat. Once the oil is hot, add the cumin seeds, cinnamon stick and green cardamom pods, and fry for 2 to 3 seconds.

Now, add the grated onion, lower the heat to medium and fry, stirring so the onion cooks evenly, until it turns slightly brown, 3 to 4 minutes. Add the chicken pieces to the pan, increase the heat to high and fry, stirring regularly, for 4 to 5 minutes. Now, add the grated tomato, tomato paste and ketchup, lower the heat to low and cook for 2 to 3 minutes. Add the slit green chiles and ginger and cook for another 2 minutes. Add the coriander, turmeric, Kashmiri red chile powder and salt to taste, and cook until the oil starts to separate from the sides of the pan, 4 to 5 minutes. Add ¼ cup (60 ml) of water if the masala is beginning to burn. Add the stir-fried onion, bell pepper and garlic back to the pan along with the garam masala and mix well. Finally, add the kasuri methi, lime juice and cilantro and mix well. Serve with pulao.

5 tbsp (75 ml) vegetable oil, divided

½ cup (80 g) thinly sliced onion

1 cup (100 g) thinly sliced green bell pepper

2 tsp (7 g) chopped garlic

½ tsp cumin seeds

1 (1" [2.5-cm]) piece cinnamon stick

2 green cardamom pods

1 cup (160 g) grated onion

1 lb (454 g) boneless chicken breast, cut into small pieces

1 cup (180 g) grated tomato

2 tbsp (28 g) tomato paste

1 tbsp (10 g) ketchup

2 green chiles, slit in half

1 tsp chopped fresh ginger

2 tsp (4 g) ground coriander

½ tsp ground turmeric

2 tsp (4 g) Kashmiri red chile powder

Salt

½ tsp garam masala spice blend

2 tbsp (4 g) kasuri methi

1 tbsp (15 ml) fresh lime juice

2 tbsp (4 g) chopped fresh cilantro

Pulao, for serving

SHRIMP MALAI CURRY

SERVES 4

Shrimp malai curry, which is traditionally known as chingri malai curry, is a silky smooth Bengali curry where shrimp is cooked in a coconut milk base flavored with sweetly scented aromatic spices. *Chingri* is "shrimp" and *malai* refers to "creamy curry"; and here the creaminess comes from the use of rich coconut milk.

I have always been a fan of seafood, and such traditional recipes have my heart. The robust authentic flavors in this Bengali dish make you go "wow" when you take its first bite. A recipe so simple yet so delicious, this shrimp malai curry is one such dish that lightens up a dull day.

You have to try this recipe if you love a good seafood curry. Rich, flavorful and delightful, it tastes heavenly on a bed of steamed rice.

1 lb (454 g) uncooked shrimp, peeled and cleaned

2 tsp (6 g) ground turmeric

1 tsp Kashmiri red chile powder

½ tsp ground cumin

1 tsp salt

¼ cup (60 ml) vegetable oil

2 bay leaves

1 (1" [2.5-cm]) piece cinnamon stick

4 whole cloves

2 green cardamom pods

2 dried red chiles

1 cup (160 g) finely chopped onion

2 tsp (6 g) ginger-garlic paste

1 tsp tomato paste

1 cup (240 ml) coconut milk

Steamed rice, for serving

In a medium-sized bowl, combine the cleaned shrimp, turmeric, Kashmiri red chile powder, cumin and salt, and toss the shrimp well with the spices. Set this mixture aside for 10 minutes.

Meanwhile, in a medium-sized, heavy-bottomed skillet, heat the oil over medium-high heat. When the oil is hot, add the bay leaves, cinnamon stick, cloves, green cardamom pods and dried red chiles to the pan, and sauté them, stirring constantly, for 4 to 5 seconds to release all their flavor into the oil.

Next, lower the heat to medium, add the onion and fry, stirring regularly, until lightly browned, 4 to 5 minutes. Once the onion is lightly browned, add the ginger-garlic paste and cook, stirring regularly, for another 2 minutes.

Now, add the shrimp mixture and sauté, tossing the shrimp regularly, for 2 minutes. The shrimp will turn pink. Finally, add the tomato paste, coconut milk and 1 cup (240 ml) of water and mix everything well. Continue to cook for 6 to 8 minutes. Serve hot with steamed rice.

DAD'S SPECIAL CHICKEN KOFTA CURRY

SERVES 4

A hearty curry prepared with a blend of wholesome spices is all you need for an exceptional meal. And what can be better than this chicken kofta curry for such meals, where beautifully flavored minced chicken meatballs are dipped into a rich tomato- and onion-based curry.

Whenever we had guests at home for a party, everyone had one request from my dad: to make one of his special curries. This curry tastes delicious with almost all Indian breads, but I prefer flaky Lachha Paratha (page 89) to go with it. You can also serve it with steamed rice.

Begin making the kofta: In a blender, combine the onion, green chiles and cilantro and blend to a smooth paste. Transfer this paste to a medium-sized bowl. Add the chicken, ginger-garlic paste, coriander, Kashmiri red chile powder, turmeric, garam masala, melted ghee, chickpea flour and lime juice and mix well to make a smooth mixture. Make balls from the mixture (about 10 to 12), wetting your hands with water while making the balls; otherwise, the mixture will stick to your palms. Set the balls aside.

Make the curry: In a large skillet with a lid (you'll need it later), heat the oil over medium-high heat. Once the oil is hot, add the bay leaf, green cardamom pods, cloves and cinnamon stick, and let them crackle for 2 to 3 seconds. Add the onion and fry, stirring regularly to cook it evenly, until it is lightly browned, 5 to 6 minutes. Add the ginger-garlic paste and fry, still stirring, until the onion turns dark brown, another 5 to 6 minutes.

Now, add the tomato puree and cook for 2 to 3 minutes. In a small bowl, whisk together the yogurt and flour. Add the yogurt mixture to the pan and cook for another 2 to 3 minutes. Whisking the yogurt with flour prevents it from curdling while cooking and also makes the curry creamier. Add the coriander, Kashmiri red chile powder, turmeric, cumin and salt to taste, and cook, stirring regularly, until the oil starts to leave the sides of the pan, 2 to 3 minutes.

Now, add 4 cups (960 ml) of water to the pan and bring the curry to a boil. Once the curry comes to a rolling boil, slide the kofta gently into the pan. Cover the pan and cook the kofta undisturbed for 4 to 5 minutes. Then, remove the lid and turn them around very gently, using a small spoon, cover and cook for another 3 to 4 minutes. Garnish the curry with chopped cilantro and serve hot with Lachha Paratha.

KOFTA

½ cup (80 g) chopped onion

2 green chiles

2 tbsp (4 g) chopped cilantro

10 oz (283 g) ground chicken

2 tsp (6 g) ginger-garlic paste

1 tsp ground coriander

1 tsp Kashmiri red chile powder

½ tsp ground turmeric

½ tsp garam masala spice blend

1 tbsp (15 ml) melted ghee

2 tbsp (17 g) chickpea flour

1 tsp fresh lime juice

CURRY

¼ cup (60 ml) vegetable oil

1 bay leaf

2 green cardamom pods

3 whole cloves

1 (1" [2.5-cm]) piece cinnamon stick

1 cup (160 g) chopped onion

2 tsp (6 g) ginger-garlic paste

½ cup (80 g) tomato puree

½ cup (120 g) plain yogurt

1 tsp all-purpose flour

1 tsp ground coriander

2 tsp (4 g) Kashmiri red chile powder

½ tsp ground turmeric

½ tsp ground cumin

Salt

2 tbsp (4 g) chopped fresh cilantro, for garnish

1 recipe Lachha Paratha (page 89), for serving

METHI FISH CURRY

I've always maintained a green patch for myself at home. I grow all kinds of vegetables, but green leafy ones and herbs are my favorite. Of spinach, fenugreek, lettuce, mint and cilantro, I usually keep a batch for harvesting every week or so. I use fresh cilantro leaves for garnishing; lettuce for my salads; and fenugreek, also known as *methi* in India, for curries as well as to mix in my dough to make parathas. Fenugreek is a very versatile ingredient and it can add amazing taste to your recipes. Here I've used fresh fenugreek leaves along with fenugreek seeds to make fish curry. This methi fish curry will be a big hit at your dinner table. You can serve it along with some steamed rice or with any Indian bread of your choice.

1 lb (454 g) fish fillets cut into 3 inch (8 cm) pieces (see Note)

1 tsp salt, plus more to taste

4 tbsp (60 ml) mustard oil

1 tsp fenugreek (methi) seeds, crushed

1 cup (160 g) finely chopped onion

2 green chiles, slit in half

2 tsp (6 g) ginger-garlic paste

½ cup (123 g) plain yogurt

1 tsp all-purpose flour

1 tsp Kashmiri red chile powder

1 tsp red pepper flakes

½ tsp ground turmeric powder

2 tsp (4 g) ground coriander

2 cups (100 g) chopped fenugreek (methi) leaves

1 tsp fresh lime juice

Wash the fish well with water and apply 1 teaspoon of salt all over it. Set the fish aside for 15 minutes. Now, wash it with water again and pat dry the pieces using a paper towel.

Make the curry: In a large skillet, heat the mustard oil over medium-high heat. When the oil is hot, add the crushed fenugreek seeds, onion and green chiles and fry until the onion turns slightly brown, 4 to 5 minutes. Add the ginger-garlic paste and fry until the onion is nicely browned and the raw smell of ginger-garlic paste is gone, another 2 to 3 minutes. In a small bowl, whisk the yogurt with the flour and add it to the pan. Adding flour to the yogurt prevents it from curdling while cooking and also makes the curry creamier. Lower the heat to medium and cook for a minute. Now, add the Kashmiri red chile powder, red pepper flakes, turmeric, coriander and salt to taste, and cook, stirring regularly, for 2 to 3 minutes, or until the oil starts to separate on the sides of the pan.

Once the oil starts to separate, add the fish pieces, fenugreek leaves and 3 cups (720 ml) of water, lower the heat to low and cook for 10 to 12 minutes. Add the lime juice and cook for another minute. Serve hot.

NOTE

You could use any fish of your choice, such as salmon, tilapia or halibut, for making this curry.

ANDA TAWA MASALA

Eggs are a rich source of protein, easy to cook and, most important, taste delicious. So, if you are someone who is fond of eggs, then this dish will be a treat for your taste buds. Boiled eggs dropped into an appetizing tomato and onion masala flavored with aromatic spices, this is a must-try for your everyday meals. If you have ever taken a road trip in India, you would have found this egg curry being served at highway restaurants and dhabas. My secret ingredient in this recipe is the pav bhaji masala, which I've combined with other spices to bring a unique taste. Quick, prepared with basic pantry ingredients and nutritious, this is a great recipe to try.

In a large *tawa* (griddle) or shallow skillet, heat the oil and butter over medium-high heat. Once they are hot, add the onion and fry, stirring, until it is slightly browned, 4 to 5 minutes. Add the ginger-garlic paste and fry for 3 to 4 minutes until its raw smell is gone. Add the tomato and cook for 3 to 4 minutes, or until the tomato is mushy; keep mashing the tomato with the back of a ladle to help it along. Once the tomato is mushy, add the coriander, Kashmiri red chile powder, turmeric, cumin, pav bhaji masala and salt to taste. Add ½ cup (120 ml) of water and mix everything well. Cook the masala until the oil starts to separate on the sides of the pan, 4 to 5 minutes.

Now, add the halved hard-boiled eggs, green chile, cilantro and lime juice to the pan, and mix everything well. Cook for 3 to 4 minutes. Serve hot with naan or paratha.

2 tbsp (30 ml) vegetable oil

1 tbsp (14 g) unsalted butter

1 cup (160 g) chopped onion

2 tsp (4 g) ginger-garlic paste

1 cup (180 g) chopped tomato

2 tsp (4 g) ground coriander

1 tsp Kashmiri red chile powder

½ tsp ground turmeric

½ tsp ground cumin

2 tsp (4 g) pav bhaji masala spice blend

Salt

4 large hard-boiled eggs, peeled and cut in half lengthwise

2 tsp (4 g) chopped green chile

2 tbsp (4 g) chopped fresh cilantro

1 tsp fresh lime juice

Naan or paratha, for serving

COCONUT MILK FISH CURRY

SERVES 4

A spicy curry bursting with the flavors from coconut milk is my weakness. No matter which cuisine it belongs to, the mere look of the curry makes me a happy person. But I lean a little more toward this recipe that is admired at home: fish pieces dunked into a spicy and creamy tomato and onion curry flavored with coconut milk. You can't miss this fish curry if you love seafood, like me. It also gets a slight tangy taste from the use of tamarind, which takes the flavor of this dish to another level. Simple and comforting, a bowl of coconut milk fish curry with some steamed rice on the side is the definition of a food coma for me.

Wash the fish fillets and set them aside.

Start the curry: Heat the oil in a medium-sized skillet over medium heat. Once the oil is hot, add the curry leaves and onion, increase the heat to medium-high and fry until the onion turns translucent, 5 to 6 minutes. Add the broken dried red chiles and green chiles to the pan and cook for another 1 minute. Next, add the ginger-garlic paste and cook until its raw smell is gone, 3 to 4 minutes.

Add the tomato and ½ cup (120 ml) of water, and cook for 2 to 3 minutes. The tomato should become mushy. Once the tomato is mushy, add the coriander, turmeric, Kashmiri red chile powder, black pepper and salt to taste. Now, add ½ cup (120 ml) of water and the tamarind paste, and cook the curry for 3 to 4 minutes. Then, add the coconut milk and bring the mixture to a boil. Once the mixture comes to a boil, reduce the heat to low and cook for another 2 to 3 minutes. Gently add the fish fillets and cook for another 7 to 8 minutes. Do not overcook the fish; otherwise, it will become chewy. Garnish the curry with fresh cilantro and serve hot with steamed rice.

NOTE

You could use any fish fillets of your choice for making this curry.

1 lb (454 g) fish fillets (see Note)

3 tbsp (45 ml) vegetable oil

20 curry leaves

1 cup (160 g) finely chopped onion

2 dried red chiles, broken into half

2 green chiles, slit in half

2 tsp (6 g) ginger-garlic paste

½ cup (90 g) finely chopped tomato

2 tsp (4 g) ground coriander

½ tsp ground turmeric

1 tsp Kashmiri red chile powder

¼ tsp freshly ground black pepper

Salt

1 tbsp (32 g) tamarind paste

1 cup (240 ml) coconut milk

1 tbsp (2 g) chopped fresh cilantro, for garnish

Steamed rice, for serving

PRIDE OF
NIZAM'S
LAMB BIRYANI
(PAGE 75)

STAPLE
RICE DISHES

I often get excited with a new rice recipe, because I simply love flavorful and aromatic rice for my meals. Even the easiest of the rice recipes tastes so good; just see my good old Cumin Peas Pulao (page 71)—so simple, yet so tasty! This was also one of the first recipes I ever learned to cook. Or you could try the more elaborate preparations of pulao or biryani.

Various kinds of rice are available in the market. In India, every region has a regional variety, such as Sona masoori in the south and Indrayani in the west. Then, there is long-grain rice; one of the most well-known varieties of long-grain rice around the world is basmati rice. Upward of 5,000 to 6,000 rice varieties are grown in India. Hence, rice is used as a staple in most homes. When you want to make every grain of rice stand out, such as in biryani, use a good-quality basmati or another long-grain rice. However, if you can get a regional variety near your location, steam and serve it along with a curry of your choice.

In this section, I've included some of the most famous Indian rice recipes that you must try. Here are some simple pulao recipes (pages 71 and 81) as well as Pride of Nizam's Lamb Biryani (page 75) and Mix Veg Biryani (page 77), and of course a Masala Khichdi (page 72), which is so light and comforting that I make it pretty often. Each recipe is so different, yet so delicious.

CUMIN PEAS PULAO
(THE FIRST DISH
I EVER MADE)

SERVES 4

A plate of simple flavored rice goes well with most Indian dal and curries. This is the first recipe I ever made, and since then, it has become one of my favorites. Whether you are planning a daily meal or something more elaborate, this easy rice recipe will always be a hit. The richness from ghee, slight flavor of cumin (*zeera*) and those soft green peas really oomph up the flavor of aromatic rice, giving us a delightful dish that tastes great with almost everything.

2 cups (370 g) uncooked basmati rice

2 tbsp (30 g) ghee

1 tsp cumin seeds

4 whole cloves

2 black cardamom pods

6 black peppercorns

2 bay leaves

½ cup (80 g) thinly sliced onion

2 drops fresh lime juice

2 tsp (11 g) salt

1 cup (130 g) frozen green peas

Wash the rice very well with water two or three times, or until the water runs clear. Soak the washed rice in 3 cups (720 ml) of water for 20 minutes.

In a medium-sized, heavy-bottomed saucepan with a tight-fitting lid (you'll need it later), heat the ghee over medium-high heat. Once the ghee is hot, reduce the heat to low, add the cumin seeds and let them crackle for 3 to 4 seconds. Slightly crush the cloves, black cardamom pods and peppercorns, add them to the pan and sauté for 3 to 4 seconds. Crushing the whole spices elevates their flavor a lot. Add the bay leaves and the onion to the pan. Fry until the onion turns slightly brown, 6 to 8 minutes. Once the onion has browned, drain the water from the rice and add the soaked rice to the pan along with the lime juice, salt, frozen peas and 4 cups (960 ml) of water. Cover the pan. Cook until all the water is absorbed and the rice is cooked perfectly, 20 to 25 minutes.

Once the rice is cooked, remove the pan from the heat and let it rest for 5 minutes. Now, remove the lid and fluff the rice gently, using a large kitchen fork. Serve with dal or curry.

MASALA KHICHDI
(MY TOP COMFORT FOOD)

SERVES 4

Khichdi has always been a comfort food in Indian homes. Traditionally, it is a combination of lentils and rice that is lightly flavored with ghee, cumin seeds, turmeric and salt. Now, how about trying a masala version of this khichdi? This one is tastier and healthier! Just the addition of some vegetables and a few more everyday aromatic spices makes it *masaledar*. You can just make it with onions and spices, but if you, like me, love your vegetables, feel free to add the vegetables of your choice. This masala khichdi is definitely a soul food when it comes to those busy tiring days, as it is super easy to make and is ready in no time.

In a medium-sized bowl, combine the rice and lentils. Wash them two or three times with water until the water runs clear. Then, soak the washed rice and lentils in 3 cups (720 ml) of water for 20 minutes. Soaking them will make sure they cook evenly and quickly.

Heat the ghee in a pressure cooker over medium-high heat. Once the ghee is hot, add the cloves, cinnamon stick, peppercorns and cumin seeds and let them crackle, stirring constantly to be sure they don't burn, for a few seconds.

Add the onion and green chiles to the pressure cooker, lower the heat to medium and cook, stirring, until the onion becomes slightly browned, 8 to 10 minutes. Next, add the ginger-garlic paste and cook for another 2 minutes. Add the potato, green peas and carrot and cook for a minute. Now, add the coriander, turmeric and Kashmiri red chile powder and cook, stirring, for a minute.

Drain the water from the rice and lentils and add them to the pressure cooker along with the salt, 4 cups (960 ml) of water and lime juice. Close the lid of the cooker and pressure cook over high heat until one whistle sounds. Now, lower the heat and cook for 10 more minutes.

Once done, remove the cooker from the heat and let the pressure release naturally. Once all the pressure has released, open the lid and mix the khichdi with a large spoon. If it is too thick, add some boiling hot water and adjust its consistency. The consistency of khichdi should be like that of porridge. Garnish the masala khichdi with fresh cilantro and serve hot with plain yogurt, roasted papad and green chutney.

½ cup (100 g) uncooked white rice

½ cup (100 g) split and skinned green gram lentils

2 tbsp (30 g) ghee

2 whole cloves

1 (2" [5-cm]) piece cinnamon stick

4 black peppercorns

1 tsp cumin seeds

½ cup (80 g) thinly sliced onion

2 green chiles, slit in half

2 tsp (5 g) ginger-garlic paste

½ cup (75 g) peeled and cubed potato

½ cup (73 g) green peas

½ cup (64 g) cubed carrot

1 tsp ground coriander

½ tsp ground turmeric

1 tsp Kashmiri red chile powder

1 to 1½ tsp (6 to 9 g) salt

1 tbsp (15 ml) fresh lime juice

2 tbsp (4 g) chopped fresh cilantro, for garnish

FOR SERVING

Plain yogurt

Roasted papad

Green chutney

NOTE

Alternatively, to make this recipe in an Instant Pot, use the sauté setting before closing the lid. Then, reducing the water measurement to 3 cups (720 ml), pressure cook on high pressure for 12 minutes, followed by natural pressure release.

PRIDE OF NIZAM'S LAMB BIRYANI

SERVES 6

Biryani originated during the Mughal era in India and has been ever so popular since then. In fact, every region in India developed a distinct way of preparing it. One of the most popular biryani destinations is Hyderabad (the land of the Nizam monarchy), which is famous for its *dum* style of cooking in a sealed container over a slow flame. If you ever visit this city in India, you will find it lined with a number of restaurants serving biryani.

I really can't think of anything that can replace a plate of biryani. The choice of rice is very important for the taste and feel of biryani. A rice grain that stands out and does not lump up after cooking is best. I usually use basmati rice for this. Biryani can be made with different meats, eggs and even vegetables. For this recipe, I've used lamb; it is cooked with a delicious medley of aromatic and flavored long-grain rice mixed with fresh herbs and crispy fried onions.

Wash the lamb with water and drain away any excess water. Place the lamb pieces in a large bowl along with the Greek yogurt, green chile paste, ginger-garlic paste, crispy fried onions, coriander, turmeric, Kashmiri red chile powder, garam masala, cumin, salt and lime juice, and mix everything well. Marinate the lamb for at least 2 hours or overnight in the refrigerator.

To cook the lamb, heat the oil in a pressure cooker over medium-high heat. Once the oil is hot, add the onion and fry, stirring frequently, until the onion turns golden brown, 6 to 8 minutes. Once the onion is browned, add the marinated lamb along with the remaining marinade in the bowl, increase the heat to high and fry, stirring regularly, for 4 to 5 minutes. Now, add 1 cup (240 ml) water to the cooker and close the lid of the cooker. Pressure cook until 1 whistle sounds, then lower the heat to low and cook for another 20 minutes. Remove the cooker from the heat and let the pressure release naturally. Once the pressure is released, open the lid of the cooker. Place the cooker back over high heat and cook until most of the water is evaporated from the lamb. Add cilantro and mint and mix well. Put the lamb aside.

Make the rice: Wash the rice two or three times with water, or until the water runs clear. Soak the rice in 6 cups (1.4 L) of water for 40 to 45 minutes. Then, heat 8 cups (1.9 L) of water in a large pot. Add the bay leaves, peppercorns, black and green cardamom pods, ghee, salt, ginger-garlic paste, green chile paste and kewra water to the pot and bring the water to a boil. Once the water comes to a boil, drain the rice and add it to the pot. Cook the rice until it is 90 percent cooked, which means that there should be a very slight bite to the rice. It will take 8 to 10 minutes for the rice to come to this stage. Once the rice is cooked to this stage, drain the water and set the rice aside.

(continued)

LAMB

2 lb (907 g) lamb pieces, bone-in

1 cup (285 g) Greek yogurt

4 tsp (8 g) green chile paste

2 tsp (6 g) ginger-garlic paste

1/4 cup (60 g) crispy fried onions

2 tsp (4 g) ground coriander

1 tsp ground turmeric

4 tsp (8 g) Kashmiri red chile powder

1 tsp garam masala spice blend

1 tsp ground cumin

2 tsp (11 g) salt

2 tbsp (30 ml) fresh lime juice

1/4 cup (60 ml) vegetable oil

1 cup (160 g) thinly sliced onion

2 tbsp (4 g) chopped fresh cilantro

2 tbsp (4 g) chopped fresh mint

RICE

2 cups (370 g) uncooked basmati rice

2 bay leaves

4 black peppercorns

2 black cardamom pods

2 green cardamom pods

1 tbsp (15 g) ghee

4 tsp (22 g) salt

2 tsp (6 g) ginger-garlic paste

2 tsp (5 g) green chile paste

2 to 3 drops kewra water (see Note on page 53)

Assemble the biryani: Transfer the cooked lamb to a large, heavy-bottomed saucepan with a tight-fitting lid. Top it with the cooked rice. Sprinkle the milk, saffron and its water, crispy fried onions and ghee on top. Now, cover the pan tightly with a lid and heat it over very low heat for 20 to 25 minutes. Remove the pan from the heat and let it rest for 10 minutes. Then, remove the lid and gently mix the lamb pieces with the rice, using a large ladle. Serve with the 5-Minute Cucumber Mint Raita.

NOTE

Alternatively, to make this recipe in an Instant Pot, use the sauté setting to cook the lamb before closing the lid. Then, pressure cook on high pressure for 20 minutes, followed by natural pressure release.

FOR ASSEMBLY

¼ cup (60 ml) milk

Pinch of saffron, soaked in 1 tbsp (15 ml) water

½ cup (60 g) crispy fried onions

2 tbsp (30 g) ghee

1 recipe 5-Minute Cucumber Mint Raita (page 140), for serving

MIX VEG BIRYANI

A medley of vegetables cooked in a spicy masala, then mixed with long-grain rice, refreshing cilantro and mint, saffron-infused milk and topped with caramelized onions, this biryani is definitely worth all the effort. Vegetables and rice are first cooked separately and then dum-cooked together, to get beautifully flavored rice that will surely cast its magic on you with its impeccable aroma. You can use the vegetables of your choice to make this dish.

Make the vegetables: In a medium-sized skillet, heat the ghee and oil over medium-high heat. Once the oil and ghee are hot, add the potato, cauliflower florets, peas, green beans and carrot to the pan, increase the heat to high and fry for 4 to 5 minutes. Transfer the fried vegetables to a medium-sized bowl.

In a separate medium-sized bowl, mix together the Greek yogurt, ginger-garlic paste, green chile paste, Kashmiri red chile powder, turmeric, coriander, garam masala, onions, lime juice, cilantro, mint, salt and oil. Pour this marinade over the fried vegetables and mix them to coat them well. Cover the bowl and set aside for an hour at room temperature.

Make the rice: Wash the rice well with water two or three times, or until the water runs clear. Soak the rice in 4 cups (960 ml) of water for 30 minutes. Then, in a large saucepan with a tight-fitting lid, heat the ghee over medium-high heat. Once the ghee is hot, add the cloves, bay leaves and cinnamon stick. Fry for 3 to 4 seconds. Drain the rice and add it to the pan along with 4 cups (960 ml) of water, the lime juice and salt. Cover the pan and lower the heat to low. Cook the rice until it is 80 percent cooked, 12 to 15 minutes; this means the rice must be almost cooked but have a little bite to it. Once cooked to the right stage, remove the saucepan from the heat.

(continued)

VEGETABLES

2 tbsp (30 g) ghee

1 tbsp (15 ml) vegetable oil

½ cup (75 g) peeled and cubed potato

1 cup (100 g) cauliflower florets

¼ cup (36 g) green peas

¼ cup (28 g) chopped green beans

¼ cup (32 g) peeled and cubed carrot

MARINADE

2 tbsp (30 g) Greek yogurt

2 tsp (6 g) ginger-garlic paste

1 tsp green chile paste

1 tsp Kashmiri red chile powder

½ tsp ground turmeric

1 tsp ground coriander

½ tsp garam masala spice blend

4 tbsp (44 g) crispy fried onions

1 tbsp (15 ml) fresh lime juice

2 tbsp (4 g) chopped fresh cilantro

2 tbsp (4 g) chopped fresh mint

1 tsp salt

1 tbsp (15 ml) vegetable oil

RICE

2 cups (370 g) uncooked basmati rice

1 tbsp (15 g) ghee

2 whole cloves

2 bay leaves

1 (1" [2.5-cm]) piece cinnamon stick

1 tsp fresh lime juice

2 tsp (11 g) salt

Assemble the biryani: Transfer the marinated vegetables to a separate large, heavy-bottomed saucepan with a tight-fitting lid, and cook for 4 to 5 minutes over high heat. Top the vegetables with the cooked rice, drizzle with the ghee and sprinkle the cilantro, mint, saffron and its milk, crispy fried onions, fried cashews and fried raisins on top. Cover the pan, lower the heat to low and cook for 15 to 20 minutes. Remove the pan from the heat and let it rest for 10 minutes. Remove the lid and fluff the biryani, using a large ladle. Serve hot with the 5-Minute Cucumber Mint Raita.

NOTE

To fry cashews and raisins, heat 1 tbsp ghee in a small skillet over medium-high heat. Once the ghee is hot, add cashews and raisins and fry for 1 to 2 minutes, until lightly browned.

FOR LAYERING

2 tbsp (30 g) ghee

1 tbsp (2 g) chopped fresh cilantro

1 tbsp (2 g) chopped fresh mint

10 to 12 strands saffron, soaked in 2 tbsp (30 ml) milk

¼ cup (50 g) crispy fried onions

10 fried cashews (see Note)

10 fried raisins (see Note)

1 recipe 5-Minute Cucumber Mint Raita (page 140), for serving

SAFFRON BASMATI PULAO

SERVES 4

Using saffron in any recipe gives a gorgeous yellowish-orange tinge that makes the recipes even more appealing. This rice pulao recipe has saffron as one of its main ingredients. Cooked in ghee, it is spiced with cinnamon and cloves, which give it an exceptional flavor. The crispy fried onions add some crunch and sweetness to the taste. Try it with some raita for the best results.

Wash the rice two or three times with water, or until the water runs clear. Soak the washed rice in 2 cups (480 ml) of water for 15 minutes.

While the rice is soaking, in a medium-sized, heavy-bottomed saucepan with a tight-fitting lid, heat the ghee over medium-high heat. Once the ghee is hot, add the cloves and cinnamon stick and fry for 20 seconds. Add the onion to the pan and fry, stirring, until it turns brown, 8 to 10 minutes. Now, drain the rice and add it to the pan. Add the salt, vegetable broth and saffron strands and gently mix everything together, using a spatula. Cover the pan and lower the heat to low. Cook until the rice has absorbed all the liquid, 15 to 20 minutes, removing the lid to stir the rice very gently once or twice while cooking, for the flavors to mix evenly. Serve hot along with the 5-Minute Cucumber Mint Raita.

1 cup (210 g) uncooked basmati rice

2 tbsp (30 g) ghee

2 whole cloves

1 (1" [2.5-cm]) piece cinnamon stick

½ cup (80 g) sliced onion

1 to 1½ tsp (6 to 9 g) salt

2 cups (480 ml) vegetable broth

20 strands saffron, unsoaked

1 recipe 5-Minute Cucumber Mint Raita (page 140), for serving

VEGETABLE CILANTRO RICE

SERVES 4

Loaded with an array of vegetables, flavored with cilantro and spiced with a few everyday Indian spices, this is something that you should definitely try for your weekday meal. It is lightly spiced and nutritious, is ready in no time and needs only a few basic pantry ingredients. Cilantro adds a great flavor and color to the rice. You can include whatever vegetables are available to you; I've used green peas, green beans and carrot. Try this simple yet delicious rice.

Wash the rice well with water two or three times, or until the water runs clear. Soak the washed rice in 4 cups (960 ml) of water for 15 minutes.

Meanwhile, in a blender, combine the cilantro, green chiles, coconut, ginger and garlic. Add ¼ cup (60 ml) of water and blend to a smooth paste. Set the paste aside.

In a medium-sized, heavy-bottomed saucepan with a tight-fitting lid, heat the oil over medium-high heat. Once the oil is hot, add the cumin seeds, cloves, green cardamom pods, cinnamon stick and bay leaves, and let them crackle for 2 to 3 seconds. Add the onion and fry, stirring, until the onion is nicely browned, 8 to 10 minutes. Now, add the coriander and Kashmiri red chile powder and fry for 3 to 4 seconds. Add the green peas, green beans and carrot, and sauté for a minute. Add the cilantro paste that you made earlier along with 3½ cups (840 ml) of water and salt to taste. Drain the water from the soaked rice and add the rice to the saucepan. Mix everything gently, using a spatula.

Cover the pan, reduce the heat to low and cook until all the water is absorbed and the rice is tender, 20 to 25 minutes. Once the rice is cooked, remove the pan from the heat and let it rest for 5 minutes. Then, remove the lid and fluff the rice gently, using a large fork. Serve hot with any raita of your choice.

2 cups (370 g) uncooked basmati rice

1 cup (16 g) packed fresh cilantro

2 tsp (4 g) chopped green chiles

¼ cup (24 g) grated fresh coconut

1 tsp chopped fresh ginger

2 cloves garlic

2 tbsp (30 ml) vegetable oil

1 tsp cumin seeds

2 whole cloves

2 green cardamom pods

1 (1" [2.5-cm]) piece cinnamon stick

2 whole bay leaves

1 cup (160 g) sliced onion

1 tsp ground coriander

1 tsp Kashmiri red chile powder

¼ cup (36 g) frozen green peas

¼ cup (28 g) chopped green beans

¼ cup (32 g) cubed carrot

Salt

Raita, for serving

LACHHA PARATHA
(PAGE 89)

MY MOST LOVED INDIAN BREADS

Indian meals would not be complete without some Indian bread. You have to serve it alongside delicious curries. If you love Indian cuisine and have been to Indian restaurants, you definitely would have tasted such breads as naan, kulcha or paratha. I'm also sure you already have a personal favorite, don't you?

In every Indian home, and if I take a bit of liberty to say at every meal, having an Indian bread or rice is kind of a tradition. I've also grown up eating roti, paratha or rice alongside a variety of vegetarian and nonvegetarian dishes. It could be a simple dal roti or sambar rice, or specials like aloo poori or paratha with a splash of butter and pickle; I've loved every combination of them.

Here in this chapter, I'll show you how you can make a variety of my most loved Indian breads in your own home, including Chile Cheese Naan (page 87), Onion Kulcha (page 93), Mix Veg Paratha (page 98), Lachha Paratha (page 89), Missi Roti (page 94) and Ajwain Poori (page 97). These generally need very basic ingredients; just follow the recipes to get to a perfect version of the bread. I'm sure you will love them.

CHILE CHEESE NAAN

SERVES 6

Naan is one of the most favorite Indian breads that goes well with Indian curries. You will find it on the menu of most Indian restaurants across the world. While it is generally made in a *tandoor* (traditional clay oven), this recipe shows you how to make it easily in your own kitchen oven. Naan can be made with no filling (usually called plain naan) or brushed with butter (usually called butter naan). It also comes with many fillings, such as *keema* (minced lamb or chicken), paneer, cheese or garlic. Here, I am sharing the recipe to make cheese naan. Soft, chewy, cheesy and spicy, it is an amazing bread to serve with your curries.

Make the dough: In a large bowl, combine the flour, milk powder, baking soda, baking powder, salt, sugar and yogurt. Mix everything well, using your fingers. Add the milk to the bowl and mix with the other ingredients. Now, add water, 1 tablespoon (15 ml) at a time, and knead to make a soft dough. The quantity of water will depend on the quality of flour you have used. To check whether the consistency of the dough is right, just press a finger on it. It should make an indentation and the dough should spring back a little. Once the dough is ready, oil a large bowl and transfer the dough to the bowl. Coat the dough all over with the oil. Cover the bowl with a clean kitchen towel and set it in a warm place for 5 to 6 hours. The dough will ferment slightly in this time and will also increase slightly in volume.

Make the filling: In a medium-sized bowl, mix all the filling ingredients and set the bowl aside. Once the dough has rested for 5 to 6 hours, it is ready to make the naan. Divide the dough into 12 equal parts and roll each part between your palms to make a smooth ball. Now, take one ball and place it on a clean surface for rolling. Dust it gently with flour and roll out, using a rolling pin, to make a 4-inch (10-cm) circle. Place 1 tablespoon (15 g) of filling in the center of the dough round and bring the edges together to make a ball again. Prepare all the dough balls in the same manner. Keep the balls covered with a clean kitchen towel until ready to bake.

(continued)

DOUGH

4 cups (480 g) all-purpose flour, plus more for rolling

1 tbsp (8 g) dry milk powder

½ tsp baking soda

1 tsp baking powder

½ tsp salt

1 tbsp (12 g) sugar

¼ cup (60 g) plain yogurt

½ cup (120 ml) warm milk

1 tbsp (15 ml) vegetable oil

FILLING

1½ cups (300 g) shredded Cheddar cheese

2 tbsp (18 g) chopped garlic

3 tsp (5 g) chopped green chile

3 tbsp (6 g) chopped fresh cilantro

2 tsp (6 g) nigella seeds (see Note)

2 tbsp (30 ml) melted salted or unsalted butter, for brushing

Preheat the oven to 400°F (200°C) and line a large baking sheet with parchment paper. Now, start to roll the naan. Sprinkle 1 tablespoon (15 g) of filling on the counter and place one dough ball on it. Dust the ball with flour and roll out, using a rolling pin, to make a 5- to 6-inch (13- to 15-cm) circle or oval. Transfer the rolled-out naan, filling-dusted side up, on the prepared baking sheet. Roll out three or four naan at a time and arrange them on the sheet. Bake the naan for 8 to 10 minutes, or until they are slightly browned on the sides. Now, change the oven setting to broil and broil the naan for 1 to 2 minutes, or until they are nicely browned on top. Remove the naan from the oven and generously brush butter over them. Prepare any remaining dough balls in the same manner. Serve hot with any curry of your choice.

NOTE

Nigella seeds, also known as black cumin and as kalonji in India, should be available in an Indian store or online on Amazon.

LACHHA PARATHA

The flaky and crisp layers formed in the paratha are called *lachha* and thus the name of this bread, lachha paratha. It is so simple to prepare, but its texture will win your heart. Aside from whole wheat flour, it also contains all-purpose flour and semolina, which help with the crispiness. This layered paratha is so appealing that it has a place on the menu of almost all Indian restaurants. While you can continue to relish it at your favorite restaurants, how about making it in the comfort of your own home? With this recipe, you will get those perfectly crisp and layered lachha parathas that can be served with delicious, rich and creamy curries.

2 cups (240 g) whole wheat flour

1 cup (120 g) all-purpose flour

1 tbsp (10 g) fine semolina

1 tbsp (13 g) sugar

1 tsp salt

2 tbsp (30 ml) vegetable oil, plus ½ cup (120 ml) for rolling and frying

In a large bowl, combine the whole wheat flour, all-purpose flour, semolina, sugar, salt and 2 tablespoons (30 ml) of oil. Add water little by little to make a soft dough. The amount of water will depend upon the quality of the flour. Do not add a lot of water at one go; otherwise, the dough can become sticky. Knead the dough for 4 to 5 minutes, or until it is soft and smooth. Cover the dough with a clean kitchen towel and set it aside on the counter for 20 minutes.

Divide the dough into 10 to 12 equal-sized balls. Take one dough ball and dust it with all-purpose flour. Using a rolling pin, roll out the dough as thinly as possible. Do not worry about the shape at this stage. Brush oil generously over the rolled dough, then sprinkle ¼ teaspoon of flour on top. Pleat the rolled dough as you might fold a paper fan. Form a pinwheel with the pleated dough. Dust the pinwheel with flour and roll it out again, using the rolling pin, to form a 6-inch (15-cm) circle.

Heat a griddle over medium-high heat. Once the griddle is hot, transfer the paratha to the hot griddle. Cook until brown spots appear on the bottom side. Flip the paratha onto the other side. Apply 2 teaspoons (10 ml) of oil to each side and cook until the brown spots darken, applying little pressure while cooking, using the back of a flat spatula. Remove the paratha from the griddle. Lightly crush from the sides to open the layers. Cook the remaining dough balls in the same manner. Serve hot with any Indian curry.

(continued)

Dough ingredients in a bowl

Soft kneaded dough

Thinly rolled dough brushed with oil and sprinkled with dry flour

Pleated dough

Pleated dough rolled into a pinwheel

Pinwheel rolled to make a circle

Paratha frying on a griddle

Lightly crushed paratha, ready to serve

ONION KULCHA

My first memories of *kulcha* go back to my childhood. It is hard to miss a kulcha on numerous roadside stalls in Punjab and Delhi. *Chole* (chickpeas) were kept in a large brass container tilted on its side along with kulcha; together they are called chole kulcha. Similar to other Indian breads, kulcha can also be made either plain or stuffed. The one I like best is onion kulcha; finely chopped onions with some spices are filled in this bread made with all-purpose flour. Pair it with spicy Pindi Chana (page 17) or any other curry, and don't forget to serve Masala Onion (page 148) and Mixed Veg Pickle (page 139) on the side.

Make the filling: In a medium-sized bowl, mix together all the filling ingredients, then set aside.

Make the dough: In a large bowl, combine the flour, baking powder, sugar and salt. Mix these ingredients well, using your fingers. Now, add water little by little and make a soft dough. The quantity of the water will depend on the quality of the flour used. Do not add a lot of water at one go; otherwise, the dough can become sticky. Once the dough is made, transfer it to a lightly floured surface. Add 1 tablespoon (14 g) of the butter to the dough and knead well until the dough is soft and smooth and the butter is completely absorbed. It will take 4 to 5 minutes of hand kneading. Alternatively, you can use a stand mixer or a food processor to knead the dough.

Spread the dough, using your fingers, to make a 9 x 13-inch (23 x 33-cm) rectangle. Brush 2 tablespoons (28 g) of the butter over the dough and fold the ends over each other. Spread the dough once again to make a 9 x 13-inch (23 x 33-cm) rectangle. Apply the remaining 2 tablespoons (28 g) of butter over the dough and fold the ends over each other again. The idea is to laminate the dough with some butter so that the resulting kulcha is very flaky. Now, bring the dough together and form it into a ball.

Preheat the oven to 400°F (200°C). Divide the dough into six equal parts and form them into balls. Cover the dough balls with a clean kitchen towel and set them aside for 10 minutes. Now, take one ball and dust it with flour. Roll it out, using a rolling pin, to make a 5-inch (13-cm) circle. Place 1 tablespoon (15 g) of the onion filling in the center of the circle and bring the ends together to make a ball once again. Roll out the stuffed dough ball to make a 5- to 6-inch (13- to 15-cm) circle. Arrange the kulcha on an ungreased baking sheet and bake for 10 to 12 minutes, or until browned on the top and sides. Brush generously with melted butter and serve hot.

FILLING

1 cup (160 g) chopped onion

1 tsp finely chopped fresh ginger

2 tsp (4 g) finely chopped green chile

2 tbsp (4 g) chopped fresh cilantro

1 tsp salt

1 tsp Kashmiri red chile powder

½ tsp ground cumin

2 tsp (4 g) dried mango powder

1 tbsp (3 g) kasuri methi

DOUGH

9 oz (250 g) all-purpose flour, plus more for dusting

½ tsp baking powder

2 tsp (8 g) sugar

1 tsp salt

5 tbsp (70 g) unsalted butter, at room temperature, divided

2 tbsp (30 ml) melted salted or unsalted butter, for brushing

MISSI ROTI

Mixing chickpea flour in small quantities with whole wheat flour is a practice in many Indian homes. I've also done it many times as it gives a different flavor to the bread. If you like chickpea flour, you should try this *missi roti*; it is prepared mainly with chickpea flour that is mixed with whole wheat flour, all-purpose flour and cornstarch to get that perfect taste and texture. This delicious missi roti is also flavored with basic spices and then topped with coriander seeds, cumin seeds, onion and cilantro. While this roti is popular at the Punjab roadside dhabas, it is equally loved in the royal state of Rajasthan, too.

Make the dough: In a large bowl, combine the chickpea flour, whole wheat flour, all-purpose flour, cornstarch, baking powder, turmeric, Kashmiri red chile powder, salt, oil, kasuri methi, ajwain, ginger and green chile. Mix the ingredients well, using your fingertips, until they all come together. Now, add water little by little and knead to make a soft dough. The quantity of water will depend on the quality of the flour used. Do not add too much water at once; otherwise, the dough will become sticky. Once the dough is ready, knead it with the heels of your hands for 2 to 3 minutes, or until it is soft and smooth. Cover the prepared dough, using a clean kitchen towel, and set it aside on the counter for 30 minutes.

Make the topping: In a small skillet over low heat, dry roast the coriander seeds and cumin seeds, stirring constantly, until they are slightly browned, 1 to 2 minutes. Once roasted, remove the pan from the heat and let them cool. Once cooled, transfer them to a mortar and pestle and crush to make a coarse powder. In a medium-sized bowl, mix this powder with the onion and cilantro. Set the topping aside.

Once the dough has rested well, make the roti: Preheat the oven to 400°F (200°C). Divide the dough into eight equal parts and form each into a ball. Place 1 teaspoon of the topping on a clean surface and place one dough ball over the topping. Now, using a rolling pin, roll out the dough to make a 4-inch (10-cm) disk, dusting with whole wheat flour as you roll if the roti is sticking to the surface. Transfer the rolled roti to an ungreased baking sheet, the topping side up. Make two to three roti per batch and place the pan on the middle rack of the oven. Bake the roti for 10 to 12 minutes, or until they are slightly browned on the top and sides. Remove the pan from the oven and generously brush the melted ghee on the roti. Prepare the remaining balls in the same manner. Serve the roti hot.

NOTE

Ajwain is also known as carom seeds; they smell like thyme and add a lot of fragrance to the recipe. You should be able to get them in an Indian store or online on Amazon.

DOUGH

1 cup (92 g) chickpea flour

½ cup (56 g) whole wheat flour

½ cup (64 g) all-purpose flour

¼ cup (30 g) cornstarch

¼ tsp baking powder

½ tsp turmeric

½ tsp Kashmiri red chile powder

1 tsp salt

2 tbsp (30 ml) vegetable oil

2 tsp (4 g) kasuri methi

½ tsp ajwain (see Note)

1 tsp grated fresh ginger

1 tsp finely chopped green chile

TOPPING

1 tbsp (5 g) coriander seeds

1 tsp cumin seeds

2 tbsp (7 g) finely chopped onion

2 tbsp (4 g) finely chopped fresh cilantro

2 tbsp (30 ml) melted ghee, for brushing

AJWAIN POORI

This ajwain poori recipe is very simple, but it has such a unique flavor that comes from ajwain (carom seeds). These tiny miracle seeds do wonders to this recipe. Believe me, there is nothing like a hot and puffed ajwain poori straight from the kadhai on your plate. This fried bread is everyone's favorite in India and you will definitely find them as a part of the festive meals. Everyone at my home loves to relish them with 10-Minute Rasedar Aloo (page 22) or Pindi Chana (page 17) for our weekend brunch. You must try out this recipe.

2 cups (240 g) whole wheat flour

1 tsp sugar

1 tsp salt

4 tsp (20 g) fine semolina

2 tsp (4 g) ajwain

3 cups (720 ml) vegetable oil, for frying, plus more for the dough

1 recipe 10-Minute Rasedar Aloo (page 22), for serving

In a large bowl, combine the whole wheat flour, sugar, salt, semolina and ajwain. Add water little by little and knead to make a stiff dough. The consistency of the dough is very important in making good puffed-up pooris. It should be a tight and hard dough.

Once the dough is ready, cover the bowl with a moist, clean cloth and set it aside for 15 minutes. The dough needs some time to rest to loosen the gluten and become soft and pliable. Once the dough has rested for 15 minutes, knead it again for a minute and then divide it into smooth 1-inch (2.5-cm) pieces. Now, flatten them a little bit in between your palms.

Take one piece of the dough and apply two to three drops of oil to it. Using a rolling pin, roll to make a 4-inch (10-cm) circle. Apply the pressure gently while rolling the poori and do not roll it too thin. The ideal thickness of the rolled poori is about 1/10 inch (2 mm). Roll four or five pooris and place them on a clean surface in a single layer.

In a medium-sized Indian kadhai (see Note), heat the oil for frying over high heat. The oil must be very hot once you start to fry the poori; otherwise, they will not puff up. To check whether the oil is hot enough, drop a small bit of dough into the oil. If it rises immediately, it means the oil is hot enough. If not, heat it for a few more minutes.

Once the oil is hot, starting from the side of the pan slip a rolled-out poori in the hot oil. Press it gently, using a slotted spatula, and fry until it puffs up, about 10 to 15 seconds. Flip it gently using the spatula and fry on the other side until golden brown. Transfer the poori to drain on a plate lined with paper towels. Similarly, fry all the rolled pooris.

To fry the next batch, lower the heat to low and roll out four or five pooris in the same manner as before. Once ready to fry, increase the heat to high and let the oil become hot. Once the oil is hot again, fry the pooris. Serve hot with Rasedar Aloo.

NOTE

You can buy an Indian kadhai from an Indian store or online on Amazon. Alternatively, you can use a Dutch oven to fry the pooris.

MIX VEG PARATHA

Stuffed paratha is a staple breakfast in Punjabi homes. Often, you will wake up to the heavenly smell of parathas frying in *desi ghee* (clarified butter), especially on weekends. Many fillings are used in paratha, such as potatoes, paneer and cauliflower. Here I've used a mixture of vegetables flavored with some basic spices for stuffing the parathas. You can use any combination of vegetables that you prefer at home. Serve it with a dollop of butter with a side of curd, pickle or chutney.

Make the dough: In a large bowl, combine the whole wheat flour, salt and oil. Add water little by little and knead to make a soft dough. The quantity of the water will depend on the quality of the flour used. Do not add a lot of water at one go; otherwise, the dough can become sticky. Knead the dough for 2 to 3 minutes, using the heels of your hands, until it becomes very smooth. Cover the bowl with a clean kitchen towel and set it aside for 20 minutes.

Make the stuffing: In a food processor, combine the cauliflower, cabbage, green beans, carrot and bell pepper. Pulse the vegetables until they are coarsely ground. Do not overprocess; otherwise, they will become pasty. Alternatively, you can chop the vegetables finely, using a knife. Transfer the vegetable mixture to a large bowl and add salt to taste. Mix everything well and set aside for 10 minutes. During this time the vegetables will release some water. After 10 minutes, squeeze the vegetable mixture well between your palms and discard the excess liquid. Add the green chile, cilantro, ginger, garam masala and chaat masala to the vegetables and mix well. Set the filling mixture aside.

Make the paratha: Lightly knead the dough once again and divide it into 6 equal portions. Form the dough into smooth balls. Now, take one dough ball and dust it with flour. Roll it out, using a rolling pin, to make a 4-inch (10-cm) circle that should be thinner around the edges. Take 2 tablespoons (30 g) of filling and spread it on the dough circle. Bring the edges of the dough together and seal them to form a ball. Press the circle slightly, dust with flour again and roll out gently to make a 6-inch (15-cm) circle. Roll the paratha from the sides to make sure the filling reaches the sides and is distributed evenly.

Heat a griddle over medium-high heat. Once the griddle is hot, transfer the paratha to the hot griddle and cook until brown spots appear on the bottom, about 30 to 40 seconds. Flip the paratha and brush with 2 teaspoons (5 g) of ghee. Flip again and brush 2 teaspoons (5 g) of ghee onto the other side as well. Press the paratha, using a ladle, and fry until it is nicely browned on both sides. Serve hot with butter, Mixed Veg Pickle and plain yogurt.

DOUGH

2 cups (240 g) whole wheat flour, plus more for dusting

1 tsp salt

1 tsp vegetable oil

Ghee or oil, for frying

STUFFING

2 oz (57 g) cauliflower, roughly chopped

2 oz (57 g) cabbage, roughly chopped

2 oz (57 g) green beans, roughly chopped

2 oz (57 g) carrot, roughly chopped

2 oz (57 g) green bell pepper, roughly chopped

Salt

1 tsp chopped green chile

1 tbsp (2 g) chopped fresh cilantro

1 tsp grated fresh ginger

½ tsp garam masala spice blend

1 tsp chaat masala spice blend

FOR SERVING

Butter

Mixed Veg Pickle (page 139)

Plain yogurt

POTATO PEA SAMOSA
(PAGE 104)

APPETIZERS AND SOUPS FOR SPECIAL GET-TOGETHERS

It's hard not to love Indian appetizers, and there is a whole range of them to try. Whether you are a vegetarian or nonvegetarian, you can look forward to a mouthwatering variety. In fact, some of them are so good and filling that I usually end up having these followed by a round of desserts, giving my main course a total miss.

These appetizers could be cooked in a tandoor or at home in an oven, like Tandoori Chicken (page 103) or Tandoori Vegetables (page 113); shallow or deep-fried in oil, such as Onion Pakora (page 106), Potato Pea Samosa (page 104) or Amritsari Machhi (page 109); or even steamed, like Veg Momos (page 114). Different cooking methods bring about a different taste, which is why I've included such a wide variety. Some of the most loved Indian appetizers are shown here, and you would surely make some people fans of Indian food if you serve them at a party.

You will also find some standard soups that have been served in India for a very long time. From a tomato soup (page 118) that is one of the most famous South Indian recipes of rasam to Mulligatawny Soup (page 121) and Lemon Cilantro Soup (page 122), you will get a feel of India with these soups made with traditional herbs and spices.

TANDOORI CHICKEN

SERVES 4

Cooking in a tandoor (traditional clay oven), which is the Indian version of barbecue, is one of the most sought-after techniques for appetizers. Of all tandoor recipes, tandoori chicken is one of the most popular ones. So, this is one recipe in Indian cuisine you just can't miss! Now, of course, your having a tandoor at home is not very probable, so I'll show you how you can make this in your home oven. My recipe will give you the exact same dish that you might have savored in an Indian restaurant. For best results, serve it with Masala Onion (page 148) and Green Yogurt Dip (page 143).

To get this recipe perfect, chicken legs with thighs are soaked in a two-step, creamy and gorgeously spiced marinating process, then roasted in the oven until you see that perfect traditional char on the top. It has a vibrant red color, due to the use of Kashmiri red chile powder and a few other spices. The taste of that spicy masala and the smoky flavor from the char on the chicken makes it irresistible. I am sure you can't just stop at one!

Wash the chicken pieces with water and pat dry, using a paper towel. Make three or four slits on each piece, using a sharp knife.

Prepare the first marinade: In a large bowl, mix together all the ingredients for the first marinade, add the chicken legs and thighs and coat well with the mixture. Cover the bowl and refrigerate the marinated chicken for 5 to 6 hours.

Add the second marinade: Remove the bowl from the refrigerator and add all the ingredients for the second marinade. Mix everything well together. Cover the bowl and refrigerate again for another 4 to 5 hours.

Preheat the oven to 350°F (175°C). Set a large roasting pan on the lower half of the oven. Set a wire rack above the roasting pan in the middle of the oven. Arrange the marinated chicken on the wire rack and roast for 20 minutes. Flip the chicken pieces, using tongs, and roast for another 15 to 20 minutes, until they are cooked well. The internal temperature of the chicken should reach 165°F (75°C) when it is cooked through. Remove the chicken from the oven and brush with the melted butter. Sprinkle the chaat masala on top. Serve hot with lemon wedges, Masala Onion and Green Yogurt Dip.

4 chicken quarters

FIRST MARINADE

1 tsp salt

2 tsp (10 ml) fresh lime juice

2 tsp (6 g) ginger-garlic paste

1 tsp Kashmiri red chile powder

SECOND MARINADE

2 tbsp (35 g) Greek yogurt

1 tsp ginger-garlic paste

1 tsp Kashmiri red chile powder

½ tsp freshly ground black pepper

½ tsp ground turmeric

½ tsp ground cumin

½ tsp garam masala spice blend

1 tsp ground coriander

2 tbsp (30 ml) mustard oil

1 tsp fresh lime juice

2 tbsp (30 ml) heavy cream

1 tbsp (4 g) kasuri methi

FOR SERVING

1 tbsp (15 ml) melted unsalted butter

1 tsp chaat masala spice blend

Lime wedges

1 recipe Masala Onion (page 148)

1 recipe Green Yogurt Dip (page 143)

POTATO PEA SAMOSA

One of the most famous street foods consumed in India is samosa. The local *halwai* (sweets and snack) shop frying about a dozen or more samosas at a time in hot oil is a treat for the eyes. These hot samosas are served with green and sweet chutney and have been a favorite since my childhood. Of course, nothing can beat these street-side samosas, but now I have this easy recipe that I use to make them at home as well. With a beautiful flaky pastry on the outside and lightly spiced potato pea masala on the inside, this samosa is a must-cook for all Indian food lovers.

Thaw the samosa patti to room temperature: Just take the packet from the freezer and let it sit on the kitchen counter for 1 hour.

Meanwhile, make the filling for the samosas: In a medium-sized skillet, heat the tablespoon (15 ml) of oil over medium-high heat. Once the oil is hot, add the asafetida, cumin seeds, fennel seeds and crushed coriander seeds to the pan and let them crackle, stirring, for 2 to 3 seconds. Add the ginger and green chile and sauté for 30 seconds. Now, crush the boiled potatoes between your palms and add them to the pan. Lower the heat to medium and add the cooked peas, kasuri methi, cumin, garam masala, black pepper, dried mango powder, Kashmiri red chile powder, coriander and salt to taste. Mix everything well, using a spatula. Keep mashing the potatoes with the back of the spatula and cook for 3 minutes. Add the cilantro and mint leaves and mix well. Remove the pan from the heat and let the filling cool completely.

Assemble the samosas: Take one samosa patti, keeping the remaining ones covered with a clean cloth, otherwise they will dry out. Now, place 1 tablespoon (15 g) of filling at one end of the patti and fold the edge over the filling to make a triangle. Keep folding the triangle over the patti until all of it is folded. Seal the edges, using water. Make all the samosas in a similar manner. Keep them covered with the cloth until ready to fry.

In a large Indian kadhai, heat the oil for frying over high heat. Once the oil is hot, lower the heat to medium and fry the samosas in batches of 5 to 6 until golden brown and crunchy, about 10–12 minutes. Transfer them to a plate lined with paper towels, to drain. Serve hot with Green Yogurt Dip.

*See photo on page 6.

24 ready-made frozen samosa patti (see Notes)

1 tbsp (15 ml) vegetable oil, plus 4 cups (960 ml) for frying

¼ tsp asafetida

½ tsp cumin seeds

1 tsp fennel seeds

1 tsp coriander seeds, crushed

1 tsp finely chopped fresh ginger

1 tsp finely chopped green chile

7 oz (198 g) peeled boiled potatoes, refrigerated for 4 to 6 hours

¼ cup (36 g) green peas, boiled

1 tbsp (2 g) kasuri methi

¼ tsp roasted ground cumin

¼ tsp garam masala spice blend

¼ tsp freshly ground black pepper

1 tsp dried mango powder

1 tsp Kashmiri red chile powder

1 tsp ground coriander

Salt

2 tsp (2 g) chopped fresh cilantro

2 tsp (2 g) chopped fresh mint

Green Yogurt Dip (page 143), for serving

NOTES

Samosa patti is available in an Indian store; it is not patties. This is similar to spring roll sheets but samosa patti is rectangular.

If you do not have an Indian kadhai, you can use a Dutch oven to fry the samosa.

Filling kept on one end of samosa

Edge of samosa folded over the filling to make a triangle

Triangle folded further

Water applied on the edges to seal the samosa

Samosa ready to fry

ONION PAKORA (A TEATIME MUST-HAVE!)

SERVES 4

A crispy pakora on a cold rainy day with a cup of hot masala chai and some spicy or tangy chutney could just be a wish come true! When it is onion pakora, it gets even better.

To me, pakoras are an emotion—an edible form of happiness. And therefore, pakoras are always on the menu for an evening with friends. When it comes to me, I just need a reason to make these. Be it a cold night, a monsoon evening or just a family get-together, you will always find me frying some hot onion pakoras in the kitchen. Thinly sliced onions dipped in spiced gram flour batter and then deep-fried until nice and crunchy, these surely will be a delight for your taste buds as well. Many street carts in India offer hot varieties of pakoras, and these are the best-selling ones. So, if you want to enjoy those same onion pakoras at home, your search for the perfect recipe ends here. Serve these with a Green Yogurt Dip (page 143) or ketchup on the side, for the best taste.

Prepare the pakora batter: In a bowl, combine the red onion, salt, Kashmiri red chile powder, ginger, cilantro, green chile and asafetida, and mash well, using your hands. Set the mixture aside for 10 minutes. During this time, the fresh ingredients—the onion, cilantro, ginger and green chile—will release water due to being mixed with salt. After the 10 minutes are up, add the chickpea flour and rice flour to this mixture and mix well, using a spoon or your hands. Now, add water, starting with 2 tablespoons (30 ml), and mix well to make a pakora batter. The consistency of the batter should neither be too thin nor too thick, just like heavy cream. Use more or less water to achieve this consistency.

Fry the pakora: In an 8-inch (20-cm) nonstick pan, heat the oil over high heat for about 5 minutes. Once the oil is hot, lower the heat to medium. Drop small pakoras, about 1 tablespoon (10 g) of batter each, into the hot oil and fry, turning the pakoras with a slotted spoon, until they are golden brown and crisp, 6 to 8 minutes. Keep the heat at medium because if the heat is too low, they will absorb oil, and if it's too high, they will get burned. Be sure to fry only 8 to 10 pakoras at a time, to avoid too much moisture in the oil and to give you space to turn them in the pan. Repeat the process for all the batter.

Drain the pakoras on a plate lined with paper towels and sprinkle the chaat masala on top. Serve the pakoras hot with Green Yogurt Dip on the side.

1 cup (150 g) thinly sliced red onion

1 tsp salt

½ tsp Kashmiri red chile powder

2 tsp (20 g) peeled and finely chopped fresh ginger

¼ cup (4 g) fresh cilantro, finely chopped

2 tsp (20 g) finely chopped green chile (see Note)

¼ tsp asafetida

1 cup (100 g) chickpea flour

2 tbsp (20 g) white rice flour

2 cups (480 ml) vegetable oil, for frying

1 tsp chaat masala spice blend

1 recipe Green Yogurt Dip (page 143)

NOTE

Decrease the amount of green chile to half if you want to make the pakoras mild.

AMRITSARI MACCHI

Punjabi food has no boundaries! From appetizers to the main course to desserts, a huge number of inviting and simply irresistible Punjabi recipes have made their place not only in India but all over the world.

While everything tastes just delicious, when we talk about appetizers, this *Amritsari macchi* is the first one that crosses my mind. It hails from the beautiful city of Amritsar in Punjab and takes its name from the city. This delectable dish is so popular in the state that you can easily find it at the roadside stalls or in the best hotels. Lightly battered and marinated fish double fried until golden brown, this starter is known for its simple recipe and impeccable taste. Marinating the fish pieces in the batter makes sure it soaks up all the flavor, delightfully resulting in this toothsome appetizer.

1 lb (454 g) fish fillets (see Note)

1 tbsp (15 ml) fresh lime juice

1 tsp ajwain

2 tsp (6 g) ginger-garlic paste

¼ tsp ground turmeric

1 tsp Kashmiri red chile powder

2 tbsp (18 g) chickpea flour

1 tbsp (9 g) all-purpose flour

Salt

¼ tsp asafetida

6 cups (1.4 L) vegetable oil, for frying

2 tsp (6 g) chaat masala spice blend

1 recipe Green Yogurt Dip (page 143), for serving

Wash the fish fillets with water and pat them dry, using a paper towel. Cut the fillets into bite-sized pieces. In a medium-sized bowl, combine the lime juice, ajwain, ginger-garlic paste, turmeric, Kashmiri red chile powder, chickpea flour, all-purpose flour, salt and asafetida and mix well to make a thick batter. Add the fish fillets to the bowl and coat them well with the batter. Divide them into three batches and set them aside.

In a medium-sized deep skillet, heat the oil for frying over medium-high heat. Once the oil is hot, working with one batch at a time, add the battered fish fillets and fry until they are slightly browned, 1 to 2 minutes per batch. Drain the fillets on a plate lined with paper towels. You can keep these aside for now and reserve the pan of oil.

Just before serving, heat the oil once again until it is very hot, and double fry the fish fillets, one batch at a time, until they are golden brown, 2 to 3 minutes per batch. Drain again on a paper towel–lined plate and immediately sprinkle the chaat masala over them. Serve hot with Green Yogurt Dip.

NOTE

You can use any fish fillet of your choice, such as tilapia, halibut or salmon.

CHICKEN SEEKH KEBAB

If you are looking for a kebab that is moist, juicy, succulent and delicious, then you should certainly attempt this chicken seekh kebab. Ground chicken meat is mixed with spices, herbs and aromatics, and then wrapped around a skewer in the shape of a log. These kebabs impart a beautiful smoky flavor, as they are traditionally grilled over a coal fire. An extremely popular appetizer made all over India, these can also be easily prepared in the comfort of your home, either in an oven or in a grill pan. They prove to be a fantastic option as an appetizer if you are planning to hold a soiree at home.

1½ oz (40 g) onion

1 lb (454 g) boneless chicken breast

2 green chiles, roughly chopped

1 tsp Kashmiri red chile powder

½ tsp ground cumin

½ tsp garam masala spice blend

½ tsp red pepper flakes

1 tsp chaat masala spice blend

1 tbsp (7 g) ginger-garlic paste

1 tbsp (4 g) fresh cilantro

1½ to 2 tsp (9 to 12 g) salt

½ tsp freshly ground black pepper

2 tbsp (30 ml) melted butter

1 recipe Masala Onion (page 148), for serving

1 recipe Green Yogurt Dip (page 143), for serving

Grate the onion, using the middle holes of a box grater. Squeeze the grated onion in between your palms and discard the liquid. Transfer the grated onion to a food processor. Wash the boneless chicken breast and pat dry, using a paper towel. Chop the chicken into small pieces and add them to the food processor as well. Add the green chiles, Kashmiri red chile powder, cumin, garam masala, red pepper flakes, chaat masala, ginger-garlic paste, cilantro, salt, black pepper and melted butter to the food processor and process to a slightly coarse paste.

Transfer the paste to a large bowl and knead it well, using your hands, for 4 to 5 minutes, or until it is very smooth. Cover and refrigerate this mixture for 3 to 4 hours.

Divide the chilled mixture into six equal parts. Take a metal skewer and insert it into one portion of the mixture. Wet your hands with water and spread the mixture over the skewer to make a 6-inch (15-cm)-long kebab. Keep wetting your hands while spreading it over the skewer. Make all the kebabs in the same manner.

Now, on a grill pan or over a barbecue grill, grill the kebabs, rotating the kebabs so they cook evenly, until golden brown on all the sides, 15 minutes. Once browned, remove them from the pan or grill and slide them off the skewer, using a fork. Serve hot with Masala Onion and Green Yogurt Dip.

TANDOORI VEGETABLES

SERVES 6

Tandoor made dishes are well known across northern India. As I mentioned earlier with Tandoori Chicken (page 103), a tandoor is a large, clay-based vertical furnace. If you visit the back room of many restaurants or some open dhabas, you will see long iron skewers threaded with vegetables, paneer or chicken, marinated in different flavors, being cooked in the tandoor.

I use a kitchen oven to make these recipes at home. In this recipe, an array of vegetables are marinated in a spicy yogurt masala and cooked to perfection. This is an amazing appetizer for vegetable lovers, perfect to make for house parties.

Make the marinade: In a large bowl, combine all the marinade ingredients, including salt to taste. Mix well to make a thick paste.

Now, add the cauliflower, bell pepper, onion, baby corn, mushrooms and baby potatoes to the bowl and coat them with the marinade paste. Cover the bowl and refrigerate the marinated vegetables for 2 hours.

Preheat the oven to 350°F (175°C). Arrange the marinated vegetables in a single layer on a baking sheet. Brush the vegetables with vegetable oil and bake for 20 minutes. Remove the pan from the oven and flip the vegetables, using tongs, and bake for another 10 minutes.

Now, set the oven to BROIL and broil the vegetables for 3 to 5 minutes, or until they are slightly blackened on top. Remove the pan from the oven and sprinkle the chaat masala over the veggies. Serve the tandoori vegetables with lime wedges, Masala Onion and Green Yogurt Dip.

MARINADE

2 tsp (10 ml) fresh lime juice

2 tsp (6 g) ginger-garlic paste

2 tbsp (35 g) Greek yogurt

1 tsp Kashmiri red chile powder

½ tsp freshly ground black pepper

½ tsp ground turmeric

½ tsp ground cumin

½ tsp garam masala spice blend

1 tsp ground coriander

2 tbsp (30 ml) mustard oil

2 tbsp (30 ml) heavy cream

1 tbsp (2 g) kasuri methi

Salt

VEGETABLES

4 oz (113 g) cauliflower, cut into medium-sized florets

4 oz (113 g) green bell pepper, cut into 1" (2.5-cm) slices

4 oz (113 g) onion, cut into 1" (2.5-cm) cubes

4 oz (113 g) baby corn

4 oz (113 g) white mushrooms

4 oz (113 g) baby potatoes, boiled until tender

Vegetable oil, for brushing

FOR SERVING

2 tsp (4 g) chaat masala spice blend, for sprinkling

Lime wedges

1 recipe Masala Onion (page 148)

1 recipe Green Yogurt Dip (page 143)

VEG MOMOS

Give me a plate full of delicious hot steamed *momos* every day, and I will eat them with joy. These steamed filled dumplings originated somewhere in northeast India; they became so famous that it was customary for anyone visiting the northeastern states to take a picture eating momos. Soon these snacks started to get sold all over India. While there are many filling variations you can make, the most sought-after are mixed veg and chicken. These are generally served with hot sauce.

Here in this recipe, an array of veggies are finely chopped, lightly spiced, stuffed into a thin sheet made out of all-purpose flour and then steamed to perfection. These veg momos are something that you definitely need to try at home.

Make the dough: In a medium-sized bowl, combine all the dough ingredients. Add water little by little to make a soft dough. Do not add a lot of water in one go; otherwise, the dough may become sticky. Cover the bowl with a damp, clean cloth and set aside for 10 minutes.

Make the filling: In a food processor, combine the garlic, ginger, onion, cabbage, carrot, green onion and cilantro, and process to a coarse mixture. Transfer the mixture to a medium-sized bowl and add the soy sauce, salt to taste, white pepper and oil, and mix well. Set the filling aside for 10 minutes. The vegetables in the filling will release water. Transfer the filling to a piece of cheesecloth and twist to get rid of all the liquid. This process will make the filling dry and the momos will not break while filling. Set the filling aside.

Now that the dough and filling are ready, assemble the momos: Knead the dough for a minute, or until it is very smooth and pliable. Divide it into about two dozen equal-sized pieces. Roll each piece in between your hands to make a smooth ball. Now, take one ball and roll it out, using a rolling pin, to make a very thin circle. Cut the circle, using a 4-inch (10-cm) round cookie cutter. Using a cookie cutter will make sure the shape of the momos is very neat and uniform. Place 1 tablespoon (15 g) of filling in the center of the circle and brush the edges with water. Bring the edges together and pleat them. Seal the ends nicely. Prepare all the momos in the same manner.

Now, heat 4 cups (960 ml) of water in a large steamer. Line up the momos in the steamer basket and steam for 15 to 20 minutes, or until they are glossy on the surface. Remove the steamer from the heat and transfer the momos to a plate, using tongs. Serve hot with a hot and sweet dipping sauce.

DOUGH

2 cups (240 g) all-purpose flour

3 tbsp (45 ml) vegetable oil

⅛ tsp baking soda

½ tsp salt

½ tsp sugar

½ tsp white vinegar

FILLING

2 tsp (7 g) chopped garlic

1 tsp chopped fresh ginger

¼ cup (30 g) chopped onion

1 cup (20 g) shredded cabbage

¼ cup (20 g) shredded carrot

¼ cup (20 g) chopped green onion

1 tbsp (2 g) chopped fresh cilantro

1 tsp soy sauce

Salt

½ tsp ground white pepper

1 tbsp (15 ml) vegetable oil

Hot and sweet dipping sauce, for serving

PALAK TAMATAR SHORBA

Soups are also known as *shorba*, a word derived from the Arabic language. In a number of Indian restaurant menus across the world, you will find the mention of shorba.

Tomato has been an ideal choice for soup in many different cuisines. Whether it's a hot summer day, a chilly monsoon evening or a super cold winter night, tomato-based soups are ever popular. Here I've mixed some spinach leaves to the tomatoes to makes the soup even more nutritious and flavorful. Spicy, sour and sweet all in one, this shorba is a fantastic choice when you crave a delicious soup. I often make this at home, as it is very easy to prepare and makes for a super comforting meal.

1 tbsp (15 ml) vegetable oil

1 tsp cumin seeds

2 bay leaves

1 (1" [2.5-cm]) piece cinnamon stick

1 tsp chopped fresh ginger

2 tsp (7 g) chopped garlic

1 lb (454 g) tomatoes, chopped

4 oz (113 g) spinach, chopped

3 tbsp (6 g) chopped fresh cilantro, divided

2 tsp (3 g) chopped green chile

Salt

½ tsp freshly ground black pepper

In a medium-sized saucepan with a tight-fitting lid, heat the oil over medium-high heat. Once the oil is hot, add the cumin seeds, bay leaves and cinnamon stick and let them crackle for a few seconds. They will release all their flavor into the oil. Now, add the ginger and garlic and fry, stirring, for another minute. Add the tomatoes, spinach, 2 tablespoons (4 g) of the cilantro and the green chile, and cook for 2 to 3 minutes.

Now, add 1 cup (240 ml) of water, salt to taste and black pepper and cover the pan. Lower the heat to low and cook for 20 to 25 minutes. Then, remove the pan from the heat, remove the lid and let the mixture cool down for 15 to 20 minutes. Once the tomato mixture has cooled down, discard the bay leaves and the cinnamon stick, using tongs.

Transfer the cooled mixture to a blender and blend until smooth. Pass the mixture through a fine-mesh sieve, pressing the mixture with the back of a spoon while passing it through the sieve. Discard the pulp that is left behind and add the strained mixture back to the pan. Add 1 cup (240 ml) of water and mix well. Cook the soup for 3 to 4 minutes over medium-high heat. Transfer to the serving bowls, garnish with the remaining tablespoon (2 g) of cilantro and serve hot.

SOUTH INDIAN TOMATO PEPPER RASAM

SERVES 4

A bowl of piping hot *rasam* on a bed of steamed rice topped with homemade ghee and fried papad on the side is a satisfying traditional South Indian meal indeed. Staying in the northern part of India, I was oblivious to rasam until a friend introduced me to this amazing preparation. Now, I make this so often that it has become part of life. This is one simple recipe from the southern part of India that you must try.

With the slight tang from the tomatoes and tamarind and the perfect hint of hotness from the pepper, this rasam is always a hit. Although rasam rice is the definition of my comfort meal, this rasam is often had just as a soup in my home, especially on those cold winter nights. It is also an excellent remedy for sick days when you get caught up with a cough and cold. It does wonders to your throat. One more reason to try this delicious tomato pepper rasam, right?

1 cup (180 g) chopped tomato

2 tsp (8 g) tamarind paste

¼ cup (18 g) cooked and mashed yellow pigeon pea lentils

4 cloves garlic, crushed

12 curry leaves

1 tbsp rasam powder

1 tsp crushed black peppercorn

1 tsp crushed cumin seeds

Salt

1 tbsp (2 g) chopped fresh cilantro

FOR TEMPERING

1 tbsp (15 g) ghee

½ tsp mustard seeds

¼ tsp asafetida

1 dried red chile, broken into 2 pieces

5 curry leaves

In a medium-sized saucepan, combine the tomato, tamarind paste, cooked pigeon pea lentils, garlic and curry leaves. Add 2 cups (480 ml) of water and simmer over low heat for 8 to 10 minutes. Now, add the rasam powder, crushed peppercorns, crushed cumin seeds and salt to taste, increase the heat to medium and cook until the rasam comes to a gentle boil, 4 to 5 minutes. Once the rasam comes to a boil, add the cilantro and mix well, then remove the pan from the heat.

To temper the rasam, in a small skillet, heat the ghee over high heat. Once the ghee is hot, add the mustard seeds, asafetida, broken dried red chile and curry leaves to the hot ghee and let them crackle for a few seconds. Pour the tempering over the rasam and mix well. Serve as a hot drink or along with meals.

MULLIGATAWNY SOUP

SERVES 4

Although you might feel it is a bit hard to pronounce, this soup is absolutely delicious. It originated in the state of Tamil Nadu and is known as a soup made with peppercorns. Being a bit thick in its consistency, it can even be used as a light stew over a bed of rice.

It gets its protein from the use of Bengal gram and pigeon peas, its creaminess from coconut milk and its flavor from ginger, garlic and spices. It also has the goodness of carrots, which makes it healthy and nutritious.

In a medium-sized pressure cooker, heat the ghee over medium-high heat. Once the ghee is hot, add the peppercorns and sauté for 3 to 4 seconds. Add the ginger, garlic, onion and curry leaves, lower the heat to medium and cook, stirring, for 3 to 4 minutes. Now, add the carrot, turmeric, vegetable stock, garam masala and salt to taste. Rinse the Bengal gram and pigeon peas and add them to the pressure cooker as well.

Close the lid of the cooker and pressure cook over high heat until one whistle sounds. Then, lower the heat to low and cook for 10 minutes. Remove the cooker from the heat and let the pressure release naturally. Once the pressure is released, open the lid of the cooker and whisk the soup, using a wire whisk. If you want a creamier soup, you can blend it in a blender or with an immersion blender until smooth. Finally, add the coconut milk and cilantro to the soup and bring it to a gentle simmer. Serve warm.

NOTE

Alternatively, to make this recipe in an Instant Pot, use the sauté setting to cook before closing the lid. Then, pressure cook on high pressure for 8 minutes, followed by natural pressure release.

2 tbsp (30 g) ghee
10 black peppercorns
1 tsp chopped fresh ginger
1 tsp chopped garlic
½ cup (80 g) chopped onion
10 whole curry leaves
½ cup (45 g) cubed carrot
½ tsp ground turmeric
4 cups (960 ml) vegetable stock
½ tsp garam masala spice blend
Salt
¼ cup (50 g) Bengal gram
¼ cup (50 g) pigeon peas
½ cup (120 ml) coconut milk
1 tbsp (2 g) chopped fresh cilantro

LEMON CILANTRO SOUP

Cilantro, known by the name *dhania* in India, is one of the most used herbs. It is used as a garnish in curries or for mixing in the masala. Here, I've used it to make lemon cilantro soup. Bursting with flavor, this clear soup is an ideal comforting dish for your dull days. While lemon adds a tangy taste, the cilantro leaves are added for their refreshing and subtle citrusy taste. Finely chopped veggies add to the flavor, making it filling and nutritious and also giving this soup a bite. Warm and satisfying, this soup is a must-try recipe.

1 tbsp (15 ml) vegetable oil

2 tsp (7 g) finely chopped garlic

2 tsp (5 g) finely chopped fresh ginger

1 tsp finely chopped green chile

¼ cup (40 g) finely chopped onion

¼ cup (23 g) finely chopped cabbage

¼ cup (23 g) finely chopped carrot

¼ cup (35 g) sweet corn kernels

½ cup (8 g) finely chopped fresh cilantro

4 cups (960 ml) vegetable stock

2 tbsp (30 ml) fresh lemon juice

2 tsp (5 g) cornstarch

Salt

½ tsp finely ground black pepper, for garnish

In a medium-sized saucepan, heat the oil over medium-high heat. Once the oil is hot, lower the heat to medium, add the garlic, ginger and green chile and sauté for 20 seconds. Add the onion and fry, stirring, for 2 minutes. Next, add the cabbage, carrot, corn and cilantro and sauté for a minute. Add the vegetable stock and bring the mixture to a boil. Now, lower the heat to low and let the soup cook for 3 to 4 minutes. Add the lemon juice and mix well.

In a small bowl, mix the cornstarch with ½ cup (120 ml) of water to make a thin slurry. Add the slurry to the pan and cook for 2 to 3 minutes, or until the soup thickens. Add salt to taste and mix well. Serve hot, garnished with the black pepper.

SAFFRON KHEER (PAGE 128)

STANDOUT DESSERTS FOR ALL OCCASIONS

What's a good Indian meal without the mouthwatering desserts? I've always had a soft spot for homemade desserts. When it is winter and carrots are in season, I look forward to my mom preparing a huge batch of gajar ka halwa. There is always some in the fridge ready to be warmed up.

Then there are a number of regional festivals, when kheer and halwa kinds of desserts are prepared. Every Indian festival has some specific desserts, which have been made traditionally using the ingredients available at that time of the year. Of course, now most of the ingredients are available throughout the year, so you can enjoy these desserts whenever you choose. Picking out a few desserts from this vast Indian cuisine was definitely a challenge, so I've included some really famous ones for you.

In addition to Indian ice cream, known as *kulfi* (page 131), this chapter offers Raisin Halwa (page 132), Saffron Kneer (page 128), a 6-Ingredient Makhana Phirni (page 135) and My Mom's Gajar ka Halwa (page 127). And since we are making desserts, let us just indulge a bit and go generous with the rich ingredients. You will love the lingering taste.

MY MOM'S GAJAR KA HALWA

SERVES 6

Gajar ka halwa (carrot halwa) is certainly not just any other Indian sweet; rather, it's a feeling for Indians. As soon as the winter arrives, sweet and juicy red carrots are available in abundance in the local markets. I make sure to get my hands on them because who doesn't love a delicious halwa for a weekend treat?

You will find this halwa being served in weddings, festivals and special occasions, where it is topped with slivered dried fruits to add a rich and royal touch to it.

The recipe I'm sharing here is time tested, having been made hundreds of times; I learned this from my mom, so this recipe is specially dedicated to her. Carrots are peeled, grated and then cooked along with sugar, milk, khoya and cardamom, until you get a delicious carrot pudding that smells divine and tastes heavenly.

1 lb (454 g) red carrots (see Notes)

2 cups (480 ml) whole milk

¼ cup (60 g) ghee

1 tsp ground cardamom

½ cup (100 g) sugar

½ cup (120 g) khoya, shredded (see Notes)

Almond and pistachio slivers, for garnish

Wash the carrots with water and peel them, using a vegetable peeler. Grate the carrots using the medium holes of a box grater. Alternatively, you can use a food processor to grate them. In a large, heavy-bottomed saucepan, combine the carrots and milk, and cook over low heat until all the milk is absorbed, 20 to 25 minutes. Once the milk is absorbed and the carrot mixture looks thick, add the ghee to the pan along with the cardamom. Cook, stirring constantly to prevent burning on the bottom, for 4 to 5 minutes. Now, add the sugar and cook for another 4 to 5 minutes. You can increase or decrease the amount of sugar per your liking. I like very lightly sweet halwa, and this measurement is perfect for that.

Once the sugar is well dissolved, add the khoya and cook, stirring regularly, for 15 to 20 minutes, or until the ghee starts to leave on the sides of the pan. Garnish it with almond and pistachio slivers and serve warm.

NOTES

I suggest using red carrots; if you do not get red carrots, you can try this with orange carrots, but the taste will not be as sweet.

While I highly recommend using khoya in this recipe, in case you are not able to find it easily in a shop near you, use 4 tablespoons (30 g) of dry milk powder mixed with 4 tablespoons (60 ml) of water.

SAFFRON KHEER

Be it a festival, wedding or any other special occasion, celebrating with something sweet is a must. It is rightly said that "a festival in India is incomplete without something sweet," and I completely agree! While many sweets are made for these occasions, kheer has been a long-standing traditional dessert across all of them.

This kheer is one of the sweets that has been made in my home for Diwali, Holi, Janmashtami and other auspicious occasions. A few strands of saffron add that beautiful yellow tinge and subtle flavor to the kheer, which makes it even more delicious and appealing. I'm sure you will love this delicious sweet from India.

3 tbsp (45 g) short-grain white rice

4 cups (960 ml) whole milk

20 strands saffron

20 whole raisins

½ tsp ground cardamom

¼ cup (22 g) desiccated coconut

¼ cup (50 g) sugar

Almond slivers, for garnish

Unsalted pistachio slivers, for garnish

Rinse the rice well with water. Soak the rinsed rice in 2 cups (480 ml) of water for 20 minutes. Meanwhile, in a large, heavy-bottomed saucepan, bring the milk to a boil over medium heat.

Once the milk comes to a boil, reduce the heat to low. Drain the rice and add it to the milk along with the saffron, raisins, cardamom and coconut. Cook, stirring regularly to prevent burning on the bottom, until the rice is softened and the milk has thickened, 40 to 50 minutes.

Now, add the sugar and cook for another 2 to 3 minutes. Never add sugar before the rice is cooked properly; it will stop it from getting softer. Mash the rice a little with the back of a ladle to make the kheer creamier.

Remove the pan from the heat and let the kheer cool down completely. Once the kheer is cooled, chill it for a few hours, then garnish with almond and unsalted pistachio slivers and serve chilled.

PISTA KULFI

Kulfi is Indian-style ice cream; I still remember the old local shops and street carts filling up aluminum or earthen pot cones with delicious flavors of kulfi and stacking them in a large earthen pot filled with ice. Over time, these have given way to modern freezers, but I just cannot forget that taste of kulfi. Pista kulfi is one cold Indian dessert that you must try.

While there can be many flavors of kulfi, the best comes with a lot of pistachios; it also adds a crunchy bite in the creamy rich kulfi, hence the name pista kulfi.

It is easy to buy kulfi molds; you can definitely find them online. While you can make this in ice pop molds as well, I would still recommend using aluminum or steel ones to get an authentic feel.

4 cups (960 ml) whole milk

4 tbsp (50 g) sugar

¼ cup (25 g) unsalted shelled pistachios, chopped

½ tsp ground cardamom

½ tsp food-grade rosewater

In a large, heavy-bottomed saucepan, bring the milk to a boil over medium heat. Once the milk comes to a boil, reduce the heat to low. Cook the milk, stirring frequently to prevent burning on the bottom, until it is reduced to half of its initial volume, 30 to 35 minutes.

Once the milk has reduced, add the sugar, pistachios, cardamom and rosewater and mix everything well. Remove the pan from the heat and let the mixture cool down to room temperature.

Pour the mixture into the kulfi molds or popsicle molds. You can use any shape and size of mold that you prefer. Freeze the kulfi overnight or for 8 to 10 hours. To remove the kulfi from the mold, dip the mold into hot water for 1 to 2 seconds and then pull out the kulfi. Cut the kulfi into slices, using a sharp knife, and serve immediately.

RAISIN HALWA

Dried fruits are used in many different recipes in India. It's easy to find curries with dried fruits as a base and a number of sweets for garnish. Interestingly they are also considered a valuable gift item in India; on such festivals as Diwali and New Year, you will find shops loaded with gift packs made with various dried fruits.

Since sweets are one of the hallmarks of Indian cuisine, I've used raisins to make this halwa, which is one of the most calorie-loaded sweets, but then you can always have cheat days and enjoy this wonderful halwa. You will notice this delectable halwa lined up on the shelves of *mithai* (sweets) shops. But I always prefer to make it at home, as it is super easy and prepared with high-quality ingredients.

You can make this on such festivals as Diwali or Holi, or include this on your party menu.

1 cup (145 g) poppy seeds

¼ cup (60 g) ghee, divided

¼ cup (40 g) almonds, finely chopped

¼ cup (37 g) cashews, finely chopped

¼ cup (37 g) unsalted pistachios, finely chopped

10 raisins

1 cup (240 ml) whole milk

1 cup (200 g) sugar

1 tsp ground cardamom

Almond slivers, for garnish

Pistachio slivers, for garnish

Soak the poppy seeds in 1 cup (240 ml) of water for 3 to 4 hours. Once they are well soaked, drain them through a fine-mesh sieve. Transfer the soaked poppy seeds to a blender along with ¼ cup (60 ml) of water and blend to a smooth paste. Set it aside.

In a medium-sized, nonstick skillet, heat 1 teaspoon of the ghee over medium-high heat. Lower the heat to medium, add the almonds, cashews and pistachios to the pan and fry them, stirring, until browned, 3 to 4 minutes. Add the raisins and fry until they plump up. Transfer the fried nuts and raisins to a plate.

Add the remaining 3⅔ tablespoons (55 g) of ghee to the same pan and heat over medium heat. When the ghee is slightly hot, add the poppy seed paste to the pan. Fry the paste, stirring regularly, until it turns nicely browned, 20 to 25 minutes. Once the poppy seed paste is browned, add the milk and cook for 2 to 3 minutes. Add the sugar, fried nut mixture and cardamom, and cook until the ghee starts to leave the sides of the pan, another 10 to 12 minutes. Garnish the halwa with slivered almonds and pistachios and serve hot.

6-INGREDIENT MAKHANA PHIRNI

SERVES 4

If you were to ask me what is my favorite Indian dessert is, I would find it rather difficult to answer your question. But the traditional classics surely have a special place in my heart, as we have been brought up relishing them during festivals and other special affairs.

Phirni is one of those desserts from the Indian heritage that has been a part of festivities in my home. A delicious and creamy dessert from the beautiful state of Kashmir, it is prepared with milk. In this recipe, makhana (fox nuts) are roasted until crisp and then crushed coarsely and added to the mixture, which is then cooked with sugar and aromatic spices to give us a beautifully flavored makhana phirni.

Now that you are familiar with this rich and royal dessert, you can include this divine makhana phirni in your festive menus.

2 tbsp (30 g) ghee

2 cups (32 g) fox nuts (see Note)

4 cups (960 ml) whole milk

12 strands saffron

¼ cup (50 g) sugar

1 tsp ground cardamom

Almond and pistachio slivers, for garnish (optional)

In a large, heavy-bottomed saucepan, heat the ghee over medium-high heat. Once the ghee is hot, lower the heat to medium, add the fox nuts to the pan and fry, stirring, until they are crisp. Once the fox nuts are roasted, remove the pan from the heat and let them cool completely for about 20 minutes. Transfer the fox nuts to a resealable plastic bag and, using a rolling pin, crush them coarsely.

Now, add the milk to the same pan and bring it to a boil over medium-high heat, stirring to prevent it from burning on the bottom. Once the milk comes to a boil, add the saffron, reduce the heat to low and cook the milk for 30 to 35 minutes, or until it is reduced to almost half of its original quantity. Add the crushed fox nuts to the pan and cook until the mixture thickens a little more. The consistency of phirni should be like that of custard. Keep in mind that it will thicken after cooling as well.

Once the phirni has reached the desired consistency, add the sugar and cardamom and cook for another 2 minutes. Remove the pan from the heat and pour the phirni into four clay serving bowls. If clay serving bowls are not available, pour it into any serving bowls that you have. Chill the phirni for 4 to 5 hours. Garnish with almond and pistachio slivers and serve chilled.

NOTE

Fox nuts are also known as popped lotus seeds; they should be available in an Indian store near you. You could also find them on Amazon.

SPICED MANGO CHUTNEY
(PAGE 147)

MUST-HAVE ACCOMPANIMENTS WITH YOUR INDIAN MEAL

Indians love to serve up a large variety of dishes. Such terms as *chappan bhog* (a selection of 56 offerings) have become synonymous with the richness of the food at special gatherings. At Indian restaurants, you are likely to see the table set up with such accompaniments as chutney, onions and pickles to go with your meal. I still remember the pickles and chutneys made in huge batches by my grandmother; they used to be distributed among the extended family.

I've tried to keep up the tradition for my family and always serve my meals with a range of preserved and fresh accompaniments. You will always find four or five varieties of pickles at my home; during summers when fresh mangoes are in season, I make mango chutney; otherwise, most regular meals are served with some kind of papad, raita, salad and beverage.

Here I've included for you a Mixed Veg Pickle (page 139) that is good with any kind of Indian meal, a Green Yogurt Dip (page 143) for serving such appetizers as tikka and kebab, 5-Minute Cucumber Mint Raita (page 140), Masala Papad (page 144), Masala Onion (page 148), one of the most famous Indian lassis (page 151) and Tangy Jal Jeera (page 152), which does wonders for your digestion.

When you are picking some recipes from the book, make sure to serve them along with these must-have accompaniments.

MIXED VEG PICKLE

Pickle is one of the most popular Indian condiments that is prepared in every region of the country. You are definitely going to find pickles in every Indian home. So, just as Indian meals are incomplete without a pickle, this book could not be done without a pickle recipe, and this mixed veg pickle is one of my favorites.

If you step into any Indian grocery store, you will find a number of pickles made with chile, lime, raw mangoes, mixed veg, garlic and many other ingredients. Although initially I used to buy them from stores, I now love to make them at home. Over many discussions with my mom and aunts, I now have a number of traditional pickle recipes up my sleeve.

This mixed veg pickle uses a range of vegetables and you can be flexible with what you use. Serve this with any of your Indian meals.

4 oz (113 g) carrot
4 oz (113 g) radish
4 oz (113 g) green mango
4 oz (113 g) cauliflower
2 oz (57 g) cloves garlic
2 oz (57 g) fresh ginger
2 oz (57 g) green chiles
½ cup (100 g) mustard seeds
¼ cup (72 g) salt
2 tsp (6 g) ground turmeric
½ cup (120 ml) fresh lime juice
2 cups (480 ml) mustard oil

Prepare the vegetables: Peel the carrot and radish, using a vegetable peeler, and cut them into ⅛-inch (3-mm) slices. Try to keep the thickness of the slices even. You can use a mandoline for this. Peel the green mango and discard the seed. Cut the flesh into 0.2-inch (5-mm) cubes. Cut the cauliflower into small florets. Peel the garlic. Peel the ginger and grate it, using the large holes of a box grater; alternatively, you can cut it into thin julienne. Discard the stems of the green chiles and cut them into 1-inch (2.5-cm) pieces; you might wish to wear gloves while handling the chiles to avoid burning your hands. Spread the vegetables on a clean kitchen towel for an hour to absorb any excess moisture. This is essential so your pickle lasts longer.

Once the vegetables are prepared, start making the masala for the pickle: In a small food processor, grind the mustard seeds to a coarse powder. Transfer the mustard powder to a large bowl. Add the salt, turmeric and lime juice to the bowl and mix everything well. Now, add the prepared vegetables to the bowl and toss everything well together, using two large spoons.

Cover the bowl loosely and keep it on the kitchen counter for 3 days so that any excess water in the vegetables evaporates, which will help the pickle stay good for a long time. After 3 days, pack the pickle mixture in a large mason jar with a tight-fitting lid. In a small saucepan, heat the mustard oil over medium-high heat until it starts to smoke. Once it starts to smoke, turn off the heat and let it cool for 15 minutes. Very slowly, pour the oil over the vegetables in the mason jar until they are covered with the oil. Close the lid of the jar loosely to allow space for moisture and gas to escape and keep it in the strong sun for 4 to 5 days. Keep shaking the jar twice daily and make sure there is no moisture in the place where you have set it.

The pickle is now ready to eat. It can be stored for 4 to 5 months in a cool, dry place.

5-MINUTE CUCUMBER MINT RAITA

SERVES 4

I have tried so many accompaniments to serve with my summer meals, but nothing beats a refreshing chilled raita. Plain yogurt gives such a soothing feeling on these hot days; don't you agree? And to make it even more interesting, I keep adding various fruits and vegetables to it, cucumber being my favorite. Cucumber, having a high water content, is considered essential to consume during summer, and thus I think yogurt and cucumber are a perfect match. The appetizing aroma of fresh mint leaves makes a bowl of cucumber mint raita even better. This raita, accompanied with an Indian dal and bread, is my go-to lunch for summer. A light meal that is wholesome, refreshing and healthy is all you need on a hot day. Plus, it's easy to assemble within 5 minutes. Do not miss serving this cucumber mint raita with your summer meals.

1 medium-sized cucumber

1 cup (245 g) plain yogurt

½ cup (120 ml) whole milk

2 tbsp (10 g) chopped fresh mint leaves

½ tsp roasted ground cumin

½ tsp black salt

1 tsp finely chopped green chile

1 tbsp (2 g) finely chopped cilantro

Wash the cucumber with water and peel it, using a vegetable peeler. Grate the peeled cucumber, using the large holes of the box grater. In a large bowl, whisk the yogurt until smooth and creamy, using a wire whisk, about 1 minute. Add the milk to the bowl and whisk well for another few seconds, or until the yogurt and milk are combined. Add the grated cucumber, mint, roasted cumin, black salt, green chile and cilantro and mix for about 30 seconds, or until everything is well mixed.

Although you may serve it immediately, for the best flavor, refrigerate the raita for an hour and serve it chilled with your Indian meals.

GREEN YOGURT DIP

This delightful yogurt-based condiment tastes heavenly with tandoori and grilled recipes. Along with the creamy texture from the yogurt, it has a refreshing flavor from cilantro and mint leaves and the perfect amount of spiciness from green chiles.

This dip, which is popularly known as *dahi* chutney in India, is effortless, healthy and quick. So, next time you make any appetizers, serve this tempting dip on the side.

In a blender, combine all the ingredients, adding salt to taste, and blend until everything comes together into a smooth paste. Serve this dip with any Indian snack or appetizer or along with the main course as an accompaniment.

1 cup (17 g) packed fresh cilantro

½ cup (8 g) packed fresh mint

2 green chiles, chopped

1 (1" [2.5-cm]) piece fresh ginger, chopped

1 clove garlic

½ cup (140 g) Greek yogurt

½ tsp ground cumin

Salt

½ tsp chaat masala spice blend

1 tbsp (15 ml) lime juice

MASALA PAPAD

SERVES 4

Who doesn't like that extra bite of crunch on the side with our everyday meals? Yes, I am talking about the popular Indian appetizer papad here. It is crunchy, quick and a nice accompaniment that makes even your simplest of meals interesting. There are many memories linked to this extremely simple papad and I must recall them here. While the raw papad was traditionally made at home, a women's cooperative organization from 1950s made it commercially popular in India; I still remember the ad's jingle being sung by a bunny, "Karram kurram . . ." promoting Lijjat papad, and of course, I can't forget the tongue twister that I enjoyed with all my friends, which went like "kaccha papad, pakka papad."

Papad is based on lentils, rice or millet. While plain fried papad goes well with a meal of khichdi or dal and rice, you will find masala papad being served as an appetizer. Masala papad became popular from Indian roadside dhabas, where they used to serve fried papad topped with finely chopped onions and tomatoes that were flavored with salt, Kashmiri red chile powder, chaat masala and lemon juice.

If you have an Indian grocery store near you, you would definitely find papad there. So, you just have to fry it and top it with masala, and your appetizing masala papad is ready to be served.

4 cups (960 ml) vegetable oil, for frying the papad

4 urad dal papad

1 cup (160 g) finely chopped onion

½ cup (90 g) finely chopped tomato

1 tsp finely chopped green chile

2 tbsp (4 g) finely chopped fresh cilantro

Salt

1 tsp chaat masala spice blend

¼ tsp Kashmiri red chile powder

2 tbsp (30 ml) fresh lime juice

In a medium-sized wide pot, heat the oil over medium-high heat. When the oil is hot, fry the papad until they puff up, holding the papad, using tongs while frying. Drain the fried papad on a plate lined with paper towels.

In a medium-sized bowl, mix together the onion, tomato, green chile, cilantro, salt to taste, chaat masala, Kashmiri red chile powder and lime juice. Arrange the fried papad on a serving plate in a single layer. Top them with this masala mixture and serve immediately.

SPICED MANGO CHUTNEY

SERVES 8

Summer is the season for mangoes in India; by some estimates, more than 1,500 varieties are grown there. The season usually starts with raw or green mangoes, which are good to use for pickle or chutney, and then moves on to the sweet ripe ones. It has been one of the most loved fruits to date.

Every Indian home usually has a pickle or chutney recipe that they make using raw mangoes, and it is customary to serve it along with most meals in the summers. So, you just can't miss this spiced mango chutney, which is spicy, sweet and sour, all at once.

This delicious condiment is prepared with raw mangoes that are flavored with spices. A chutney can up the game of a simple meal, so try this one today!

1 lb (454 g) raw (green) mangoes

3 tbsp (45 ml) vegetable oil

½ tsp asafetida

½ tsp nigella seeds

2 tsp (4 g) fennel seeds

2 tsp (12 g) salt

2 tsp (6 g) Kashmiri red chile powder

1½ cups (225 g) jaggery, crumbled (see Note)

Prepare the mangoes: Wash them well with water and then peel away the skin, using a sharp paring knife. Now, cut off the flesh around the seed and discard the seed. Grate the green mango flesh, using the large holes of a box grater.

In a medium-sized skillet with a tight-fitting lid (you'll need it later), heat the oil over medium-high heat. When the oil is hot, add the asafetida, nigella seeds and fennel seeds and let them crackle for 3 to 4 seconds. Add the grated mango, salt and Kashmiri red chile powder and mix everything well. Add 1 cup (240 ml) of water and cover the pan. Cook for 3 to 4 minutes, or until the mango flesh is softened. Now, add the jaggery and cook until it melts, 4 to 5 minutes. Let it cool and store in an airtight container in the refrigerator for up to a month. Serve with any Indian meal.

NOTE

Jaggery should be available in an Indian store or online on Amazon. Alternatively, if it is not available, you can use coconut sugar instead.

MASALA ONION

A mild, sweet taste and the bite from the raw onions really add to the flavor of a meal. Onions have had a longtime romance with Indian dishes, as you might have seen throughout this book; they have been used in most of the recipes. Even raw onions have been served on the side of Indian meals since time immemorial. I serve raw onions in multiple different ways at home, from just simply sliced to masala onion to onions dipped in vinegar, and so on.

Here, I'll give you one of the simplest onion recipes to make your meal truly Indian. Masala onion goes very well as an accompaniment to most meals and even with such appetizers as Tandoori Chicken (page 103), Amritsari Machhi (page 109) or Chicken Seekh Kebab (page 110). The raw onions are sliced and jumbled together with spices and lime juice to give us a spicy tangy side dish that can be ready in under 5 minutes.

2 large red onions, cut into thin rings
½ tsp salt
1 tbsp (15 ml) fresh lime juice
½ tsp Kashmiri red chile powder
½ tsp chaat masala spice blend

Place the onion slices in a bowl and use your hands to separate the rings from one another. Add the salt, lime juice, Kashmiri red chile powder and chaat masala and mix everything well. Refrigerate the masala onion for 30 minutes. Serve fresh.

MANGO CARDAMOM LASSI TO COOL YOU DOWN

India lies in the tropical region and it gets super hot and dry during summer. Lassi was served traditionally to help people bear this hot and dry weather. It also keeps you hydrated, and its cooling properties give you instant relief from the scorching heat outside. Lassi is one of the most delicious beverages served in India and it should be on your must-make list.

Also, if you are having regular Indian food with many spices, it is important to cool down on a regular basis. There is nothing better than this delicious lassi to do that. Yogurt helps your stomach cool down and heal up; it is also the primary ingredient of this beverage, so you must try it out. It is refreshing, healthy and will surely brighten your day with its incredible taste.

2 cups (490 g) plain yogurt

2 cups (400 g) ripe mango, peeled and cubed

2 tsp (8 g) sugar

½ tsp ground cardamom

6 medium-sized ice cubes

1 cup (240 ml) whole milk, plus more if needed

Mint, for garnish

This recipe is very easy to make: In a blender, combine the yogurt, mango, sugar, cardamom, ice cubes and milk and blend until everything comes together. Add some more milk if the lassi is too thick for your liking. Pour the lassi into serving glasses and garnish with mint. Serve chilled.

TANGY JAL JEERA

Jal jeera is known for its digestive properties and it goes well before or with your meals. It gets its green color from mint and cilantro leaves, tanginess from the use of lime juice and dried mango powder, while cumin and asafetida do the magic with digestion.

Jal jeera has been served for decades all over India. So, get the ingredients together, make this delicious beverage and enjoy its refreshing taste and healthful properties.

Wash the mint and cilantro leaves until the water runs clear. Drain the excess water and transfer the leaves to a small food processor. Add the ginger and ¼ cup (60 ml) of water and process to a smooth puree. Transfer the puree to a large glass jug. Now, add the remaining ingredients and 4 cups (960 ml) of water to the jug and mix everything very well. Make sure to chill the jal jeera for at least 3 to 4 hours before serving. To serve, give it a stir and pour into serving glasses. Serve chilled.

½ cup (15 g) tightly packed fresh mint leaves

½ cup (15 g) tightly packed fresh cilantro leaves

1 (½" [1.2-cm]) piece fresh ginger, chopped

2 tbsp (30 ml) fresh lime juice

½ tsp roasted ground cumin

¼ tsp asafetida

2 tsp (11 g) black salt

2 tsp (11 g) salt

¼ tsp freshly ground black pepper

1 tsp sugar

2 tsp (8 g) dried mango powder

1 tbsp (30 g) tamarind paste

INDIA'S MOST
FAVORITE
PANEER
MAKHANI
(PAGE 14)

ACKNOWLEDGMENTS

There are so many people who have helped me and influenced me over the years in my cooking journey and to write this book directly or indirectly. Along the way, I've learned many things, done many experiments and overcome many obstacles. I also believe that there is still a long way to go. Making recipes and helping people experience food was not something I just dreamed of one day; it has taken years to shape up. Thanks to all of you who have been part of my adventure.

I want to thank my mom and dad who made our school lunch boxes with new interesting recipes and instilled a love for food in me over many years.

Thanks to my partner, Mohit, with whom I started to travel the world and came across cuisines and a variety of food that I'd only read about. Together we got to experience so many new recipes that I re-created at home and which eventually became my blog, Whisk Affair. Mohit has been my rock for the last 17 years. He has always been a supportive and believing partner. My blog and this book would not have been possible without his support.

This book took a lot of effort in terms of researching, cooking, shooting and compiling, and I want to thank Deepali and Malvika for helping me through this journey.

My house helps Shobha and Sujata, who had done so much extra over the days when I was trying and perfecting these recipes; they were ever smiling and helpful.

My son, Bhavye, who helps critique many of my recipes until they get to perfect. My siblings and extended family Shivangi, Shashank, Devina, Rohit, Roopali and Shobhit, who always encourage me. My beagle, Oreo, who is my most faithful cheerleader; he never leaves my side and accompanies me around the house during all my work.

My extended family, aunts, uncles, cousins and numerous friends who appreciate my work constantly and motivate me to do more.

To readers of my blog, Whisk Affair, who over the years have loved my recipes and sent me so many wonderful personal notes appreciating my work; you are a big reason I came to write this book.

Thanks to Marissa and the team at Page Street Publishing, for believing in the idea of this book and bringing it to life with super amazing efforts, guiding me all along the way.

This book is just one more way I want to help people like you experience food and, in specific, Indian cuisine. Thanks to you for picking up a copy; I'm sure you will love the recipes.

ABOUT THE AUTHOR

Neha was born to doctor parents in the small town of Banda in the state of Uttar Pradesh in India. She grew up across the state, moving with the transferable job of her parents. She studied to be a dental surgeon in Lucknow, completing her long-standing ambition to be a doctor herself. However, she didn't take to working in clinics as a long-term profession. Being creatively oriented, she wanted to explore the world and do something different; soon, she gave up her career in dentistry to pursue other opportunities. She got a chance to travel and stay for long in many different parts of the world and learn the regional culture, beliefs and food over many years. She has stayed in India, Malaysia, Czech Republic and the United States, traveling extensively in and around these countries.

Neha always had a passion for food from her childhood, and the exploration led her to try many recipes from across the world. She started to create them at home and write them down as she perfected them in a blog. Blogging was still new when she started off, and her recipes were well appreciated by her friends and family. She took pride that her recipes always turned out good every single time as they were properly measured and cooked. Her blog, Whisk Affair, started to grow from here, and so did the fan base of her recipes. Over the years, she has become an expert at making new recipes, and her readers trust her tried and tested recipes. Neha believes consuming food has changed in meaning over the years; people across the world are becoming more and more open to trying new recipes from across borders, and she loves to help them experience food.

You, too, can follow Neha and her recipes on her blog, Whisk Affair.

TANDOORI VEGETABLES
(PAGE 113)

INDEX